Make or Break

How the Next Three Years Will Shape South Africa's Next Three Decades

Richard Calland

Published by Zebra Press
an imprint of Penguin Random House South Africa (Pty) Ltd
Reg. No. 1953/000441/07
The Estuaries No. 4, Oxbow Crescent, Century Avenue, Century City, 7441
PO Box 1144, Cape Town, 8000, South Africa

www.penguinrandomhouse.co.za

First published 2016

1 3 5 7 9 10 8 6 4 2

Publication © Penguin Random House 2016
Text © Richard Calland 2016

PUBLISHER: Marlene Fryer
MANAGING EDITOR: Robert Plummer
EDITOR: Bronwen Maynier
PROOFREADER: Lisa Compton
COVER DESIGNER: Gretchen van der Byl
TYPESETTER: Monique van den Berg
INDEXER: Sanet le Roux

Set in 11.5 pt on 16.5 pt Adobe Garamond

Printed by **novus print**, a Novus Holdings company

This book is printed on FSC® certified and controlled sources.
FSC (Forest Stewardship Council®) is an independent, international, non-governmental
organization. Its aim is to support environmentally sustainable, socially
and economically responsible global forest management.

ISBN 978 1 77609 076 1 (print)
ISBN 978 1 77609 077 8 (ePub)

Make or Break

For Rebecka

Contents

Preface
and acknowledgements

I SAY IN THE introduction to this book that there is something
rather mesmerising about watching a big, powerful political
party suffer a resounding electoral setback – as the ANC did in the
2016 local government elections held on 3 August. You can all but
taste the shock and then, almost simultaneously, the denial. What
are the five stages of grief? Denial, anger, bargaining, depression
and acceptance. This book was finished in the immediate aftermath of that election result, when the process had already reached
the 'bargaining' stage, as the coalition discussions unfolded behind
closed doors. Their outcome, crucial as it will be for the future of
South African politics, was unknown when we went to print. So the
question of what particular combinations of parties would form
governments in Nelson Mandela Bay and the metropolitan councils

tion, a decision was rightly taken to hold publication until after the results became available. That meant a rather frantic rewrite not only of the chapter on the election, but also of various other sections in the book, such was the impact of the results, so that it could still be brought out in record time.

My earlier draft of Chapter 4 began confidently: 'The 2016 local government elections will be a game changer.' At least I was right about that. Indeed, I had been saying as much for at least three or four years. The writing was on the wall: the ANC, with its rotten leader, had lost its way, and the electorate was onto them. South Africa, it turns out, has a robust, multiparty, competitive democracy after all. And the game-changing quality of the election results was even more striking than anticipated. The people spoke, and with a sharp tongue.

But what will happen now? Will it nudge South Africa's political trajectory onto a more positive plane or will it simply serve to disappoint, masking the underlying, stubborn structural economic obstacles to progress and prosperity? There is hope and uncertainty in equal measure across the nation. On one level, the election result changes nothing. The grave socio-economic conditions remain; the absurd power struggle at the heart of government – between the president and his minister of finance – endures. On another level, it changes everything. ANC hegemony has been penetrated. How the ruling party will react is just one of several key questions that this book examines.

As such, it is very different from my two previous books on South African politics – *Anatomy of South Africa* (2006) and *The Zuma Years* (2013) – which were compasses, not maps. They sought to dissect the body politic and to explain how power worked. This book looks ahead, and seeks to forecast. It is therefore more of a map, offering inflection points to look out for, like signposts, as well as identifying the big questions and issues that will, over the coming three years, shape the next thirty – the book's core thesis.

The idea was conceived in the early hours of a cold Berlin morning a couple of weeks after my daughter Ivy Anouk was born at the end of 2015, as I walked her up and down trying to persuade her to sleep. It is a good time to think. The next day I was due to fly to London to speak to the clients of an investment bank about South African politics and I was running through my main points in my head. It suddenly occurred to me that I should write it all down in a short, crisp, accessible book. I wrote to Marlene Fryer and Robert Plummer at Zebra Press, and they responded almost immediately with gratifying enthusiasm.

As with *Anatomy of South Africa* and *The Zuma Years*, they have been marvellously supportive, as well as trusting: agreeing to take the very unusual step of editing the chapters as they rolled off my laptop and into the inbox of my superb editor, Bronwen Maynier, who did as expert a job with this book as she did with *The Zuma Years*, only under greater pressure. I am very grateful to her, and to Robert and Marlene.

I should also acknowledge and thank Lawson Naidoo and Ian Farmer, my cofounding partners of the political-economy consult-

volume are mine and mine alone.

Lastly, this 'pamphlet', as she amusingly likes to refer to it, is dedicated to my partner, Rebecka, mother of our daughter, Ivy.

RICHARD CALLAND
CAPE TOWN, AUGUST 2016

Abbreviations and acronyms

ACDP: African Christian Democratic Party
ANC: African National Congress
BEE: black economic empowerment
CASAC: Council for the Advancement of the South African
    Constitution
COPE: Congress of the People
COSATU: Congress of South African Trade Unions
DA: Democratic Alliance
DGRU: Democratic Governance and Rights Unit
EFF: Economic Freedom Fighters
GCIS: Government Communication and Information System
ICC: International Criminal Court
IEC: Independent Electoral Commission
IFP: Inkatha Freedom Party
IMF: International Monetary Fund

NPA: National Prosecuting Authority
NPC: National Planning Commission

OCJ: Office of the Chief Justice
PAJA: Promotion of Administrative Justice Act
SAA: South African Airways
SABC: South African Broadcasting Corporation
SACP: South African Communist Party
SAHRC: South African Human Rights Commission
SARS: South African Revenue Service
SCA: Supreme Court of Appeal
SOE: state-owned enterprise
UCT: University of Cape Town
UDM: United Democratic Movement

INTRODUCTION

Game on!

How Zuma's grave 9/12 miscalculation reset South Africa's political trajectory

I T WAS AROUND 10:30 p.m. on 4 August 2016 when the penny began to drop for the leadership of the African National Congress (ANC). At the Independent Electoral Commission (IEC) national results operations centre in Pretoria, a crisis meeting was hastily convened. Four of the ANC's most powerful people gathered in the area where each political party is given one small desk with one desktop computer – in the world of the IEC, all parties are equal. ANC deputy secretary-general Jessie Duarte had been there for hours and the strain was starting to show; she was becoming increasingly irascible. Towering over her diminutive figure, the suave treasurer-general, Zweli Mkhize, surveyed the carnage on the big electronic scoreboard above them as it revealed the big hits the

The room they found was indeed quieter, away from the hurly-burly of politicos and journalists milling around the main area, but it had windows, like a goldfish bowl. They were joined by loyal apparatchik Andries Nel, deputy minister for cooperative governance and traditional affairs, the department responsible for local government. Minutes earlier, Mantashe had stood joking with Economic Freedom Fighters (EFF) Dali Mpofu and Floyd Shivambu. Now there was no trace of a smile as Nel flicked repeatedly on his iPad, briefing the stony-faced group – which included three of the ANC 'top six', Mantashe, Mkhize and Duarte – on the emerging car wreck of an electoral result.

I could not take my eyes off of them; there is something totally mesmerising about seeing a big, powerful political party in a state of shock after it has suffered a resounding electoral setback. 'It's a crisis meeting,' admitted one of the people who had led the ANC's campaign, but who was now excluded from the conversation. 'It won't be the last. We have been given a lot to think about.' 'We've had worse moments,' the likable ANC chief whip, Jackson Mthembu, reminded me as he passed by shortly afterwards. 'And we always bounce back.' But will they? 'They're finally admitting that he is a liability,' observed United Democratic Movement (UDM) leader Bantu Holomisa. 'The only question is whether they can find a way to remove him.' The 'he' is Jacob Zuma, the leader of a ruling party whose share of the national vote has fallen 10 per cent from the previous local government elections in 2011, and 8 per cent from the national election in 2014, to just under 54 per cent in a stunning result that is guaranteed to inject new life into South African electoral politics.

But how did we get here? The origins of this significant loss of power, specifically Zuma's, and the resultant 'reset' of South Africa's political trajectory, reach back to December 2015 …

They may now find themselves in different political parties, but Yunus Carrim and Floyd Shivambu have more than their party political origins in common: they share a wicked sense of humour and contrarian instincts. The one remains a loyal though singularly independent-minded member of the ANC; the other is a strident, muscular presence in Parliament as one of the first batch of economic Freedom Fighters elected in the 2014 national election. In mid-December 2015, the two men found themselves sharing an underground train in London. Like his leader, 'Commander in Chief' Julius Malema, Shivambu is a constant thorn in the side of the ANC, the political party that expelled him back in 2013. Carrim, who was briefly in the cabinet during Jacob Zuma's first administration, is now chair of the Standing Committee on Finance in the National Assembly, on which Shivambu also serves.

The finance committee was on a study visit to the UK, hence the shared ride on the Tube. Another of their number, Des van Rooyen, was not with them. But for the fact that he was such an innocuous member of the committee, he would have been conspicuous by his absence. Van Rooyen had notified Carrim of his withdrawal

They often hear the gossip before anyone else. Shivambu had been told that Zuma was about to sack respected finance minister Nhlanhla Nene and replace him with Van Rooyen. As Wednesday 9 December drifted along, Shivambu began to tease Carrim between meetings that it was about to be announced. Carrim laughed it off with his trademark giggle. Impossible, he thought. Impossible was what a lot of people thought. Only one person thought it possible and that was the man who thought he had the power to do it: Jacob Zuma.

Back in Cape Town, Zuma chaired the last cabinet meeting of the year. It was unexceptional and the president gave no indication of the drama that was about to unfold. In London, Carrim's phone began to hum. Recognising the numbers of experienced political journalists such as *Business Day*'s Carol Paton, Carrim could tell that it was the media who were calling him. By now beginning to suspect that Shivambu had actually not been joking, Carrim chose not to answer his mobile. After all, what could he say? That he had not known it was coming? That he was as shocked as anyone? That it was completely ridiculous?

Everyone remotely interested in politics in South Africa has a 'Where were you when you heard?' story about the political event that is now called '9/12'. In Cape Town, for instance, former finance minister Trevor Manuel and his wife, Maria Ramos, the former Treasury director-general under Manuel and now CEO of ABSA, were having a quiet dinner out together, as they like to do whenever their respective schedules allow. When they heard the news they immediately headed home to comb social media, checking their Twitter feeds constantly as they drove, trying to gauge the reaction, nearly all of which was a combination of shock and anger.

While Manuel made calls to trusted friends within the ANC,

Ramos began to plot with colleagues in ABSA and the finance sector more broadly. Both groups – key people within the ANC, and senior corporate leaders in the finance sector – were to play a critical role in the drama that was to unfold over the coming four days.

For my part, I was in Europe. As usual, I had attended the international climate-change negotiations conference that in 2015 was taking place in Paris. Assuming that my working year was all but done, I got on a train with my two older children and headed south towards the Italian Alps. Unable to connect to the WiFi on the train, I switched off my phone. When we arrived at our hotel mid-evening and I turned on my phone, I was aghast at what confronted me. For the first time, I was not only furious but also bleak. If the president could make such a self-evidently dangerous, self-serving and thereby reckless and irresponsible decision, *and get away with it*, then it seemed to me that South Africa was heading to a very dark place. There was a strong suspicion that Zuma was appointing a pliant finance minister who would rubber-stamp illegitimate public expenditure and turn a blind eye to public procurement irregularities. But the question was: could he get away with it?

I remained grumpy for the next four days, my holiday now disturbed by the need to stay in touch with what was happening back home, commenting in the media, speaking with my corporate client

with a completely unheard-of backbench member of Parliament was an event of similar proportion for South African politics. Certainly, it will continue to reverberate for years to come. Its ramifications have already had a profound impact on the course of politics in South Africa, as well as on government–business relations, which, ironically, given the damage that 9/12 did to the economy, business confidence and the climate for investment, are now 'better and more productive than they have been for fifteen years', in the words of the CEO of one of the big four South African banks with whom I discussed the impact of 9/12.

Ultimately, 9/12 will be Zuma's undoing. After a fraught four days, during which the markets battered South Africa's currency and its government bonds, Zuma was forced to reshuffle the pack, bringing Van Rooyen's short-lived stay at Finance to an abrupt end, and replacing him with the highly respected Pravin Gordhan, Nene's predecessor as finance minister, on Sunday 13 December.

In years to come, when he is gone, it will be possible to trace Zuma's loss of power to 9/12. Because that day he lost his political bearings and broke two of the great rules of South African politics, one of them universal, the other particular to the ANC. First of all, politics being the 'art of the possible', Zuma attempted the impossible. In the event, he could not get away with it. Secondly, the main reason he could not get away with it was that his decision to fire Nene without consulting the rest of the leadership of the ANC broke a cardinal rule of ANC convention and culture.

That evening, when ANC secretary-general Gwede Mantashe was asked by the media for the ANC's reaction to the decision, Mantashe pointedly replied: 'The ANC has no response because the ANC was not consulted.' He was furious then, and he remains angry now. Mantashe and Zuma had already fallen out, but 9/12 turned Mantashe into a political enemy. Ever since, Mantashe has been plotting Zuma's downfall. It is a question of when, not if.

This may surprise many readers of this book, most of whom will have watched events unfolding over the early months of 2016 and concluded, in dismay, that Zuma's grip on power was holding, not slipping. After all, he survived not only 9/12 but also the Constitutional Court's seminal judgment that he, along with Parliament, had violated the Constitution in failing to implement Public Protector Thuli Madonsela's remedial action in the case of her report on the president's private homestead, Nkandla: namely, to pay back (some of) the money. That judgment was handed down on 31 March 2016. The next day, April 1st, Zuma went on live television to offer an 'apology' in which he disingenuously reframed the sequence of events since Madonsela published her report 'Secure in Comfort' in March 2014. It was so insincere, and so riddled with untruths, that it suggested Zuma was still unable to face up to the fact that he was under enormous pressure, wounded and weakened, and hanging on to power by his fingernails. If the sense of crisis at the top of government was not so serious, one might have thought: ah, yes, good one, you got me there JZ, great April Fool joke!

The man, it would appear, has the skin of a rhino, and is appar-

to Zuma, Mantashe appeared to be relishing his moment in the limelight. In a previous book (*The Zuma Years*) I compared the role of Mantashe as secretary-general of the ANC to that of a traffic policeman, in these terms:

> There are certain junctions or roundabouts in certain cities – usually busy cities in developing countries in Latin America, Africa and Asia – where, buried amid the cacophony of cars arriving at all angles, there stands a traffic officer with pristine white gloves. While all around there is madness, those crisp white gloves stand out as a beacon of order.
>
> In terms of the ANC, that traffic officer is Gwede Mantashe – a smart, streetwise, equable (mostly), approachable (often) and jocular (nearly always) character, a 'paid-up member of the human race', with a sense of humour and rhino-thick skin, who doesn't seem to take criticism personally, and who is impossible to dislike even when he is defending the indefensible with a contorted logic that defies any form of mental gymnastics.
>
> The fundamental purpose of his position as secretary-general is to manage the traffic. And the ANC is a very busy, very messy and very noisy roundabout. Sometimes, the white gloves are obeyed, sometimes not. But without them, a greater chaos would ensue.[1]

On Friday 1 April 2016, Mantashe managed the traffic with great aplomb, giving lectures to journalists for over an hour on ANC institutional procedure and democracy, and defiantly pronouncing that the ANC 'would not play to the gallery' by recalling Zuma just because the opposition were calling for it. Making reference to the dramatic 'recall' of Thabo Mbeki in September 2008, Mantashe asked rhetorically: 'Do you really expect us to tear ourselves apart like that again?'

So, to the uninitiated, it might appear as if Mantashe was pulling up the drawbridge in defence of his president and thereby defending the indefensible. But that would be a misreading: what Mantashe was doing was pulling up the drawbridge *to defend the ANC* – a very different proposition. In fact, to those of us more accustomed to having to read between the lines, what Mantashe was also signalling, not completely subtly, was that he and much of the rest of the ANC were executing a strategy of containment in respect of Zuma. Mantashe, for instance, welcomed the fact that Zuma had earlier 'humbled' himself before the nation, and on more than one occasion he pointed out to the assembled press that the ANC 'does not pivot around one leader'. If anything, Mantashe is the pivot around which the ANC rotates. His handling of the traffic, and his handling of the strategy of restraining and not – yet – recalling Zuma, reveal a great deal about the state of the ANC and what will happen next.

A second key moment in the rollercoaster ride of the final months of 2015 and the first quarter of 2016 was when, on 16 March, Mcebisi Jonas, the deputy minister of finance, decided to go public and confirm that he, extraordinarily and outrageously, had been approached by members of the Gupta family who, in effect, offered an ANC figure speaking 'truth to power' with such penetrating and probative effect. It was another 'Where were you?' moment.

I was driving back to Johannesburg from Sun City, the some-what surreal and incongruous setting for Bank of America Merrill Lynch's annual emerging-markets conference, where my fellow cofounders of the Paternoster Group, Lawson Naidoo and Ian Farmer, and I had taken a forcefully bullish line on the trajectory of South African politics. Using our narrative that 9/12 had acted as a dramatic reset, and that things would never be the same again, we argued in the face of considerable and understandable scepticism from the sharp-nosed analysts and investors with whom we had met in one-on-ones for two whole days, that although it would not be a smooth linear story, and that there would be serious setbacks as events unfolded, Gordhan and his group of reformers would win the war even if they lost battles along the way. So when I got a text message from Naidoo, who was travelling in a different car, saying that Jonas had made a public statement, I anxiously held my breath. I feared that Jonas had done what countless other ANC politicians during the past two decades had done and put out a statement denying a Gupta approach and expressing his support for President Zuma. That he did no such thing was important, showing not least that Treasury was united behind Gordhan and no less determined to protect its institutional integrity. But even more important was the fact that it provided such clear evidence of the attempted 'state capture' that the reform group was finally beginning to challenge.

A few days after Jonas's admission, a less publicised set of on-the-record comments made by Themba Maseko, the former head of the Government Communication and Information System (GCIS), was quoted at length in the *Sunday Times*. In the article, Maseko gave a detailed and devastating account of the Guptas' dealings, directly linking Zuma to the infamous family:

Maseko said that in late 2010, he received numerous requests from the Guptas for a meeting.

On the day he finally agreed to meet them at their Saxonwold home, he received a call from the highest office in the land.

'As I am driving out of the GCIS building [in Pretoria], I got a call from a PA from Mahlamba Ndlopfu, saying: "Ubaba ufuna ukukhuluma nawe [The president wants to talk to you],"' said Maseko.

'He came on the line. He greeted me [and] said: "Kuna labafana bakwaGupta badinga uncedo lwakho. Ngicela ubancede [The Gupta brothers need your help. Please help them],"' he said.

With this account, Maseko is the first top official to directly link Zuma to lobbying for the Guptas to get business from the state.[2]

I recall Maseko from when he first got the GCIS post. He is an unassuming man, with a reassuring, quiet disposition. He is generally well liked and respected by the media. He is not prone to hubris or exaggeration. He is unlikely to have gone public purely in service of any particular faction. He most likely did it because it was the right thing to do and he felt it was time to speak out.

The combined effect of Jonas's and Maseko's evidence is useful in terms of the containment strategy that Mantashe is seeking to execute. Recognising that the balance of forces within the ANC's national executive committee (NEC) still probably falls in Zuma's favour, Mantashe has to bide his time. Nevertheless, in the wake of an NEC meeting held a week after Maseko's revelations in the Sunday press, Mantashe announced that he would be conducting an investigation into 'state capture by the Guptas and others', saying that members of the ANC were to come to him with evidence. Mantashe had put himself at the centre of this process, with the aim of controlling what happens next. When the time was politically ripe, he would be able to provide the accumulated evidence against Zuma. But the president continues to enjoy the support of a majority of NEC members, and he appears to have pulled off a vigorous fight-back campaign, not for the first time in his chequered political career, and probably not for the last. Mantashe was pushed into retreat at the ANC's late May 2016 NEC meeting, on the basis that only one (Themba Maseko) of the eight people who had originally come to him with information relating to 'state capture' by the Gupta family had handed in a written submission. Consequently, it looks increasingly like Zuma will survive at least until the ANC's December 2017 national elective conference.

Eventually, Zuma will go. Whenever that is, whether sooner or later, it will not be pretty. The ANC is confronted with a deep-seated division that threatens to tear it apart. Yet it is a tremendously resilient organisation. It has often had to bring itself back from the brink. But make no mistake, despite the decisiveness of its 2014 national election victory – winning again, for the fifth time in a row since the first democratic election in 1994, over 60 per cent of the popular vote – its grip on power is slipping, as the results of the 2016 local government elections revealed with stunning effect. In addition to Cape Town, which it lost in 2006, the ANC was pushed under 50 per cent in the political, governmental and economic heartlands of the country – namely, Nelson Mandela Bay, Tshwane (Pretoria) and Johannesburg – and forced to negotiate with smaller opposition parties, which it had been able to summarily ignore and dismiss for two decades.

* * *

This book is largely about what happens next and what it will mean for the future, because how the ANC responds to this seismic shift in its hold on political power will have a huge impact on the future of the country. South Africa has entered a new era of competitive politics and coalition government. The ANC, and the country for that matter, has virtually no real experience of coalition government. How the leadership of the various political parties – especially the ANC, the Democratic Alliance (DA) and the EFF – cope with the particular complexities of coalition arrangements will matter a great deal not only to how those cities are run, but also to the internal politics and future of the various parties. The serious setback that it suffered at the polls on 3 August may jolt the ANC back to its senses or it may instead prompt it, for example, to choose a far more muscular and populist leader as a successor to Zuma, whose own departure from the scene may be hastened by the bad result, as the ANC comes to recognise that he has become an electoral liability. This might, in turn, be very bad for Cyril Ramaphosa's prospects of finally securing the big prize. It will certainly feed directly into the ANC's succession battle and the race for victory at its next five-yearly national elective conference at the end of 2017 and then, beyond, at the next national election in 2019. As this book went to print, just two weeks after the 2016 local government elections, all bets were off. What could be said with certainty, however, was that things would never be the same again.

The impact on policy and governance should not be under-estimated. If the ANC panics, it may set it – and the government – onto a different, more populist or nationalist path, with severe consequences for the country's future. In the past, the ANC has, with its alliance partners the Congress of South African Trade

Unions (COSATU) and the South African Communist Party (SACP), but especially the trade union movement COSATU, operated as a 'sponge', soaking up much of the socio-economic, system-level pressures on South Africa, thereby underpinning its ability to maintain social order and economic stability. Under Zuma's rule, the ANC has become more divided and COSATU has broken up and weakened. It is a shadow of its former self.

But for Zuma himself, and his many infelicities and scandals, this would have been the biggest political story of the last seven years. The impact of the weakening of COSATU, the consequent change in its relationship with the ANC and the alliance as a whole, and, in turn, the effect on industrial relations and collective bargaining – most obviously represented by the tragic events leading up to the Marikana massacre – have had far-reaching political and socio-economic consequences. Instead, it has been all about Zuma and the political economy of the group of 'predators' who have, with his approval, held the state 'captive', thus infecting the heart of government with the disease of corruption.

And yet, as 2016 unfolded, so, thanks in part to the catalytic effect and 'wake-up' call of 9/12, new battle lines were drawn and the moderate, social democratic/sensible left of the ANC finally found its voice. Fronted by finance minister Pravin Gordhan but with Mantashe's crucial backing, this group has mustered the courage to stand up to Zuma and his cronies. How this ongoing battle for control of government and the execution of the reform package that Gordhan unveiled in his February 24th Budget Speech play out will have far-reaching implications for South Africa's economy and its people, because these factors will be decisive not just in terms of market and investor sentiment, but in determining whether South Africa is downgraded by the rating agencies in December 2016. Such an outcome will have disastrous negative consequences for the economy and on the livelihoods of the poor, leading, in turn, to social unrest and widespread violence.

For the DA, the municipal elections were a big test of Mmusi Maimane's leadership and the (entirely rebuttable) proposition that a black leader was necessary to take the DA 'to the next level', to use the cliché. The DA was under great pressure to show serious headway in terms of both votes and seats in councils, but also some level of progress in securing substantially more black voters if they were to offer a more credible national-level challenge to the ANC in 2019. They largely succeeded on all fronts. The DA is, more or less, on track. And for the EFF, it was the opportunity to prove that they are more than the flash in the pan that all of the party political start-ups since 1994 have been. My view was that they would need to add at least 5 per cent to the 6.35 per cent they commendably achieved from a standing start in 2014 but, ideally, would need to have their votes sufficiently concentrated to win enough seats in councils in order to be kingmakers in any coalition negotiations. They achieved the latter but not the former. Despite getting a greater proportion of the votes (just under 2 per cent more, increasing nationally from 6.35 per cent to 8.24 per cent), they added barely 100 000 votes. Nevertheless, putting themselves in the position of kingmaker was probably, on balance, more useful to them than sheer weight of votes. How they play their cards now, and whether underneath it all they can sustain their militant brand, will also be a very important issue for the character and trajectory of South African politics for the next phase of its democratic consolidation ... or disintegration.

* * *

In this book I identify six critical questions, the answers to which will impact on South Africa's future and have profound long-term consequences. What are the questions?

1. Will the judiciary and other key institutions such as the public protector continue to be able to enforce the rule of law and thereby hold the line against executive abuse of power? (Chapters 1, 2 and 3)

2. Having made serious inroads into ANC hegemony in a game-changing set of local government elections in August 2016, can the opposition kick on and make the most of their progress, and what will be the likely implications for the opposition, for the ANC and for a new era of coalition politics? (Chapter 4)

3. How will the ANC respond to the election results, who will succeed Zuma and when, and what will it mean for policy in the future? Could the ANC and thereby South Africa's policy and regulatory environment shift in a more populist or nationalist direction? (Chapter 5)

4. Will Jacob Zuma in any case be reprosecuted for corruption and, if so, when? (Chapter 6)

5. Can Pravin Gordhan survive and succeed sufficiently to execute Treasury's reform package? (Chapter 7)

6. What will happen if Gordhan fails or falters? What will be the impact of a rating-agency downgrade in December 2016 and could South Africa face a Brazil-like crisis? Will the centre hold? (Chapter 8)

The quality of the rule of law and the strength of judicial independence are two of the big indicators that influential market analysts and opinion-makers will look at, and where this book heads first.

Much of *Make or Break* is concerned with such indicators. The aim is to equip readers to assess not just the future prospects of South Africa in general, but the landmarks/signposts that they should be looking out for over the coming three years.

The last few years have understandably seen a lot of negative sentiment towards South Africa. Much of it is self-imposed; some of it is not. As Ian Farmer, the former CEO of Lonmin and the cofounding partner of my political-analysis consultancy the Paternoster Group, often puts it in discussion: this is not a great time for the world economy; it is an especially difficult time for emerging markets; and it is not a good period for South Africa and mining in general. He is prone to add that it is especially horrible for precious metals, such as platinum. When trade and industry minister Rob Davies says, as he regularly does, that 'we have to operate in circumstances that are not of our making', this is what he means. He is not, in fact, looking for soft excuses. Rather, he is lamenting how much is beyond the control of most governments in the modern era.

It is a delicate time in a difficult year. The world appears especially precarious and its markets particularly volatile. And in South Africa, as the effects of the most recent drought kick in and food prices rise, more protests are likely, probably encouraged and accompanied by a vigorous student movement, and a perfect storm of political, social and economic circumstances may converge. How the political leadership responds, and how these events shake and shape the other key political landmarks of the next three years – from the municipal elections in 2016, through the ANC's national conference in 2017, to the national election in 2019 – will have profound, long-term consequences for the economy and the people of

South Africa. Thus, the next three years will set the course for the next thirty. There are real opportunities and cause for optimism, and reasons to be cheerful, but there are also grave dangers and cause for great concern. It really is make-or-break time.

1

The last frontier

Can the judges hold the line?

I N JANUARY 2015 a London-based asset manager told me, 'I have taken a big chunk of cash – $300 million – out of Russia … and put it into South Africa.'

Why would a financial expert do that? Because he trusts the rule of law here and therefore has faith that 'the CEOs and senior executives of the companies I invest my clients' money in are not going to be arrested suddenly'. That is why he was taking the cash out of Russia. 'I don't trust Putin at all; he does this shit, all the fucking time.' So South Africa is a safer bet? Yes: for all his many faults, I don't think Zuma is going to do any of that shit.

Although I am not entirely convinced, frankly. The security state around Zuma has increased significantly. Perhaps not surprisingly, given his professional history as the head of the ANC's intelligence arm during the struggle against apartheid, Zuma's approach is often influenced by the securocrats, with spooks loyal to Zuma making their presence felt within the bitter feuds that scar the face of today's ANC. When a long-time senior ANC friend of mine visited for a chat in early 2016, despite the fact that we have trusted each other for many years, he not only requested that I put my phone on flight mode but insisted on doing it himself (third-party cellphones are used for espionage purposes). Political assassinations have gone up exponentially. Zuma is ruthless and brave, as everyone who knew him in the old days tells me. And as 9/12 so powerfully revealed, he has apparently lost his political bearings and is capable of reckless acts that he believes will serve his narrow interests and those of the people close to him, but which are dangerous and harmful to South Africa's interests. So, regardless of the efforts of the reform group led by finance minister Pravin Gordhan, we are in a very risky, potentially highly unstable period.

Almost anything is possible at the hands of this president.

The big question is: are the institutions of democratic account-ability up to the job of protecting the Constitution and the public interest from Zuma's vandalism? Overall, I believe they are.

At times, these institutions look like they, too, may be a part of the collateral damage of the Zuma years. Battered by the strong head-winds of an uncongenial global economy and unable to make much progress in escaping the clutches of the stubborn structural con-straints embedded within the domestic economy, ANC leaders in government have lashed out at softer targets more readily within reach, such as the judiciary. This is why I refer to the judiciary as the 'last frontier'. Actually, it was Hassen Ebrahim, the wily bureaucrat nominated in mid-2016 to become a human rights commissioner – a very good idea – who first used the phrase at the time he was assisting Chief Justice Sandile Ngcobo in his far-sighted process of building a substantial Office of the Chief Justice (OCJ). Ebrahim was the CEO of the Constitutional Assembly back in the mid-1990s. His book *The Soul of the Nation* is a seminal and appropriately detailed account of the wonderful process of constitution-making, a process whose legitimacy is now being questioned by nationalists within the ruling party and militant young students who choose to see the Constitution as a neo-colonial construct that is hindering rather than helping 'transformation'. Ebrahim's desire to serve Ngcobo was informed by a fundamentally important proposition: in any democracy, but especially a constitutional democracy where the judicial branch of government is given the power and authority to override the 'political' (i.e. elected) branches – Parliament and the executive (government) – the independence and strength of the judiciary is vital.

Market analysts and investors, such as my asset-manager friend back in January 2015, recognise this too, although they may have somewhat different motives: they want to know that their clients' money will be safe, and that assets will not be nationalised or otherwise appropriated without due process of law. This is why they, too, pay attention to the rule of law and are highly sensitive to any perceived threats to judicial independence.

In this regard, the last few years have been a rollercoaster ride in judicial–government relations.

So, how strong is the rule of law in South Africa? Will it, and the other key institutions of democratic governance – such as the public protector, to whom I return later – hold? Although its leadership would deny this, the ANC has blown hot and cold over the Constitution. Why is this? It reflects the party's own ambivalence about constitutional democracy, the system of government which it chose. To return to basics for a moment, the thing about a constitutional democracy that can really stick in the craw of a democratically elected government, especially one with a big majority like the ANC, is that the bottom line stops with the courts: it is unelected judges who decide what is and is not constitutional, and that gives them the power and authority to countermand those who have been elected, which can be jolly irritating to the latter group.

This feature of contemporary South African politics, which is not likely to go away anytime soon, has revealed itself in many different ways in recent times. There have been covert, and sometimes overt, attacks upon the constitutional settlement of 1994 and the final Constitution that was written immediately thereafter and which until recently has enjoyed high levels of legitimacy and widespread acceptance within broader South African society – attacks that have been taken up by some elements of the student protest movement. To find an exceptionally clear expression of this attitude, which has strong nationalist overtones, one need look no further than the op-ed piece penned by cabinet minister Ngoako Ramatlhodi in 2011:

> We thus have a Constitution that reflects the great compromise, a compromise tilted heavily in favour of forces against change. However, there is a strong body of thought arguing the view that our Constitution is transformative. In this regard, a point needs to be made that a constitution can either be progressive or reactionary, depending on the balance of forces in the society it governs. In our case, the black majority enjoys empty political power while forces against change reign supreme in the economy, judiciary, public opinion and civil society. The old order has built a fortified front line in the mentioned forums. Given massive resources deriving from ownership of the economy, forces against change are able to finance their programmes and projects aimed at defending the status quo. As a result,

formal political rights conferred on blacks can be exercised only within the parameters of the old apartheid economic relations. This imbalance is reflected across the length and breadth of the country in economic, social and even political terms to some extent. The objective of protecting white economic interests, having been achieved with the adoption of the new Constitution, a grand and total strategy to entrench it for all times, was rolled out. In this regard, power was systematically taken out of the legislature and the executive to curtail efforts and initiatives aimed at inducing fundamental changes. In this way, elections would be regular rituals handing empty victories to the ruling party. Regarding the judiciary, a two-pronged strategy is evident. The first and foremost is to frustrate the transformation agenda by downplaying requirements of gender and colour representation ... The other tactic is to challenge as many policy positions as possible in the courts, where the forces against change still hold relative hegemony. The legislature itself has not escaped the encroaching tendency of the judiciary, with debatable decisions taken by majority views, in some instances.[1]

As I have written elsewhere in response to this threat to the Constitution and the concern about the gap between the promise of the Constitution and the lived reality for the majority of people in South Africa:

Stripped to its bare essentials, this line advances the following set of propositions: black people are still very poor compared with white people; white people are using institutions such as the judiciary to frustrate change and the transfer of economic

power; the Constitution is to blame for this because it contains
political compromises that are exploited now by white interests
… When there is doubt about the legitimacy of the Constitution, then certain people or interest groups will exploit the
weakness to further their own anti-democratic agenda.[2]

Progressive thinkers have hit back against the crudeness of populist
approaches such as that advanced by Ramatlhodi, describing it as
'insane' and 'dangerous',[3] and as rendering the Constitution vul-
nerable to what Sipho Pityana, the chairman of AngloGold Ashanti
and the founding chairman of the Council for the Advancement
of the South African Constitution (CASAC), has described as a
potentially destabilising assault by populist factions within the ruling party.[4]

Disregard for the Constitution also showed itself in the Nkandla
case, a case that alongside 9/12 has had a huge impact on the recent
and immediate future course of South African politics. When the
public protector, Thuli Madonsela, filed her now famous report
on Nkandla – 'Secure in Comfort' – in March 2014, she had to do
so in Parliament, because it is Parliament who appointed her and
it is Parliament to whom she accounts. Parliament duly tabled the
report and an ad hoc committee was established to consider it.
What the committee should have focused its attention on – as the
opposition, to a man and woman, argued – was how best to ensure
that the executive take the remedial action that the public protector had recommended. The phrase 'take remedial action' is now
well known. It comes from section 182 of the Constitution and has
given rise to a certain amount of confusion. President Zuma and
his legal team exploited any uncertainty about its precise meaning

to their full advantage, albeit in an entirely disingenuous way, to try to explain away his refusal to take the main piece of remedial action that he was supposed to take: namely, to pay back (at least some of) the public money that had been unlawfully spent on Nkandla (a figure, it later transpired, of R7.8 million, as determined by Treasury pursuant to the Constitutional Court's order that it should decide how much Zuma pays back).

But, when the ad hoc committee began its work in spring 2014, it became almost immediately apparent that the ANC members of the committee had not the slightest intention of ensuring that Zuma take the action that the public protector's report clearly required him to take. What the ANC's attitude revealed was the real and emerging fault line in contemporary South African politics: the ruling party's growing contempt for the Constitution and its increasingly muscular complaint about counter-majoritarianism – the idea (usually expressed as a 'dilemma' in academic literature) that there is an innate and difficult tension in a constitutional democracy when the majority is constrained by the rules from doing what it might otherwise please. At one point, Mathole Motshekga, the leader of the ANC group on the ad hoc committee and a former chief whip, asked rhetorically in words to this effect: how can the public protector be treated as more important than we who have been elected to Parliament by the people? Motshekga must be a singularly poor lawyer or a particularly cynical politician – or possibly both – not to know the answer to this. In constitutional law terms, it is very simple: the Constitution is supreme and so a constitutional body such as the public protector has greater authority.

During the transition to democracy in the early 1990s, South Africa turned its back on its system of parliamentary sovereignty and chose instead to be a constitutional democracy. The ANC was fully behind this decision. It did not want a repeat of the executive abuse of power that had characterised the apartheid era. Having made its bed, now it has to lie in it and, apparently, it no longer finds it so comfortable.

Of course, while the legal answer to Motshekga's question is absolutely and categorically clear, decisive and comprehensive, it does not provide a satisfactory *political* answer. Notwithstanding the Constitution, what the ANC is really pointing to is the counter-majoritarian impact of the Constitution and its various institutional manifestations, whether in the form of the courts overturning government law or policy, or the public protector ordering 'remedial action' to be taken by the executive that is not to the president's liking. At the time, I wrote in my *Mail & Guardian* column: 'This is why the litigation that will inevitably flow from the choice that the ANC has made in the ad hoc committee should focus not just on whether the Public Protector's "remedial action" is binding or whether the committee was legally "irrational" in declining to either get legal opinion on the point or to call Zuma to give evidence before it, but on the bigger question of Parliament's role and authority in such matters and in a constitutional democracy more generally.'[5] I turned out to be partly right: there is no doubt that the Constitutional Court's judgment in the Nkandla case was remarkable, not only because it stood up so strongly to the president, but also because it gave Parliament a very firm *klap* for failing to support the public protector and hold the executive to account.

The gravity of the Constitutional Court's judgment in the Nkandla case cannot be overstated. When the highest court is required to rule on a serious constitutional violation by a sitting president, it is always a matter of the highest order and the ultimate test of the independence of the courts, which is why I return to deal with the issue extensively in the next chapter. For the moment, however, the last word should go, somewhat ironically given his political background, to Freedom Front leader Connie Mulder. Shortly before the opposition walked out of the ad hoc committee on the principled grounds that the ANC was wholly undermining the Constitution – as the court later found – he gave, in my opinion, one of the finer parliamentary speeches of the modern era, which, addressing the ANC, ended with words to this effect: 'You may think that when you try to defend the interests of your president you are doing the right thing. But you are wrong. And the Constitution will prevail.'

Mulder was right. The Constitution did prevail. But the question we have to keep coming back to is this: will it continue to prevail? If investors and analysts, such as the asset manager at the outset of this chapter, continue to believe that South Africa's rule of law and its constitutional institutions are robust, then they are far more likely to have confidence in South Africa and its economy. South Africa's rule of law, and the quality of its courts, judges and legal system in general, is a major comparative competitive advantage. As such, it needs to be preserved and nurtured, not undermined. Which is why the ANC's pathetic, small-minded parochialism over Nkandla, and other similar matters, is so short-sighted and dangerous. It has prompted them to make a series of unjustified attacks upon the judiciary, which in mid-2015 led the judiciary to call for a meeting between its leadership and the government.

The meeting was requested after a series of public comments

by leading members of the government and the ruling ANC that Chief Justice Mogoeng Mogoeng described as 'gratuitous'. The statement from the judiciary, presented in defiant terms by Mogoeng at the press conference that followed an extraordinary meeting of senior judges, expressly recognised that the judiciary is not beyond criticism: 'Judges like others should be susceptible to constructive criticism. However, in this regard, the criticism should be fair and in good faith. Importantly the criticism should be specific and clear. General gratuitous criticism is unacceptable.'[6]

Gratuitous criticism from the government and from senior members of the ANC has become more common in recent years. Legitimate engagement with the reasoning of specific judgments was absent, for example, from this ANC alliance statement read by Gwede Mantashe: 'There are already commonly expressed concerns that the judgments of certain regions and judges are consistently against the state, which creates an impression of negative bias.'[7] Likewise, reasonable critique is not apparent in the bare allegation that there is an 'anti-majoritarian liberal offensive' seeking 'regime change' in which the courts are frequently being used to challenge the ruling alliance precisely because the judiciary is 'the least transformed part of the state'.[8] Minister of police Nkosinathi Nhleko has also alleged that some judges have met with people 'to produce certain judgments'.[9]

But the straw that broke the proverbial camel's back as far as Mogoeng and his senior colleagues were concerned was when the government blatantly misled the court, and then disobeyed its order to arrest Sudanese president Omar al-Bashir. The fugitive from international law for crimes against humanity was in South Africa to attend an African Union summit in June 2015. Zuma issued a proclamation granting al-Bashir immunity, but, as the court said, this could not trump either the statute affirming South Africa's ratification of the International Criminal Court (ICC) treaty or the court's own order that the ICC arrest warrant be executed by the South African government.[10] As the government's advocate played for time in court, al-Bashir was happily flying back home, rendering the judgment of the Pretoria High Court an exercise in futility, enraging the usually mild-mannered judge president of the division, Dunstan Mlambo, and prompting the call for the extraordinary meeting of the leadership of the judiciary and the subsequent request for a sit-down with government.

The blandness of the joint statement that emerged afterwards disguised the drama and tension of the day-long meeting, during which the ANC chose to don its most cynical and deliberately gauche political clothes. Each of the eight senior ministers present had been given a specific role and was fully prepared, initially catching the chief justice and his eight fellow senior judges off guard.

Housing minister Lindiwe Sisulu, for example, attacked the judiciary on the basis of a contorted logic which says that because independent civil society organisations such as Section 27, the Socio-Economic Rights Institute of South Africa and CASAC litigate against the state, they must be 'enemies of the state' and, since these devious, unpatriotic organisations have former Constitutional Court judges such as Yvonne Mokgoro, Zac Yacoob and Kate O'Regan on their boards, so, too, these judges must be 'enemies of the state'. Hence – in a breathtaking display of paranoia and misjudgement – Sisulu asked: should we not conclude that they were enemies of the state when they were sitting judges?

Cyril Ramaphosa, once the proud steward of the constitution-making process, took on the job of chief attack dog against Chief Justice Mogoeng Mogoeng, spending a cringe-worthy thirty minutes or more taking the country's senior judge line by line through some off-the-cuff remarks that he had made at the University of the Witwatersrand, which had been miraculously recorded and transcribed (again, evidence of the heavy, and partisan, hand of the intelligence services). Minister of science and technology Naledi Pandor, who also should know better, took aim at Mogoeng's deputy, Dikgang Moseneke, by once again dragging up the remarks he made at his private birthday party not long after the ANC's national conference in Mangaung in late 2012 and to which the ANC took thin-skinned offence.[11]

Sometime after the extraordinary meeting, minister of justice Michael Masutha, who ordinarily is a decent and sensible man, went public with a complaint against former judges being associated with litigating non-governmental organisations (NGOs). As is the case with Ramaphosa and Pandor, Masutha must know that this is brainless hogwash – that judges, once freed from their duty to be careful about what they say when they are on the bench, enjoy full freedom of speech and association rights thereafter – but presumably felt compelled to descend towards the gutter to show his loyalty to a president whose pathological use of political power to secure his own interests apparently knows no bounds. Now there are rumours that the government is preparing legislation to limit the activities of NGOs that are funded by foreign donors. As a public-interest lawyer friend wryly observed to me, 'The law is already drafted ... back in 1976. They just have to find it and dust it down!'

At the August 2015 extraordinary meeting, Mogoeng did not back down. He won the admiration and respect of many of those present who had reason in the past to doubt his strength and resolve. Many, of course, expected him to be a lapdog chief justice, a poodle in the big paws of the man who had appointed him, Jacob Zuma. I did not necessarily expect that. My concern, expressed at the time of Mogoeng's appointment in September 2011, in terms that I do not retreat from or regret, was that he simply was not up to the job. I ended my chapter on the judiciary in my last book, *The Zuma Years*, with these admittedly unkind words: '... a president who doesn't read appoints a chief justice who doesn't write. It makes perfect sense.' At the time, I did not think that Zuma had especially wanted Mogoeng to succeed Sandile Ngcobo as chief justice, mainly because Mogoeng was not the ANC's or the president's first choice. After they abandoned Ngcobo, they tried at least two, maybe three, other people. Supreme Court of Appeal (SCA) president Lex Mpati and Constitutional Court judge Sisi Khampepe were asked, but they declined. Mpati likes his life in the Free State, not far from his Eastern Cape farm, and is close to retirement. Unlike Mogoeng, Khampepe modestly thought that she was too new on the Constitutional Court to lead it. The government requested research on the judicial records of five people: Mpati, Khampepe, Bernard Ngoepe, Kenneth Mthiyane and Dunstan Mlambo. And then, a

should not have been appointed and that Moseneke, or one or several other more eminent jurists, should have got the job. The

Constitutional Court is weaker as a result. Mogoeng has been a far from perfect leader of the court, allowing, at one point, too many justices to be away on various kinds of leave, resulting in him having to appoint four acting judges. This was inappropriate and caused great unhappiness within the court, and undermined the authority of some of the judgments adjudicated by the court during the period when there were four acting justices.

Nonetheless, Mogoeng has shown leadership, partly because of his determination to continue the far-reaching project to create real administrative autonomy from the executive branch of government that had been commenced so ably and wisely by his predecessor, Chief Justice Sandile Ngcobo,[12] but also, notably, in his judgment in the Nkandla matter. Perhaps the government expected him to be a poodle, a soft touch. If so, it has been sorely disappointed and surprised. More than one old legal hand has made reference to the famous story about apartheid-era prime minister John Vorster speaking about his own partisan approach to judicial appointments in the following rather amusing way: 'Yes, they are our people, but the problem is that after six months they begin to believe that they were appointed on merit.' Mogoeng has spoken up for the judiciary on numerous occasions, not least at the explosive meeting with the executive in August 2015, winning him the respect of many of his colleagues, including his deputy chief justice, Dikgang Moseneke, who, upon his retirement from the Constitutional Court on an emotional occasion at the end of May 2016, publicly told Mogoeng, '... your integrity has been shown to be beyond questioning ... I am happy to tell our people that yours are safe hands.'

That the government was getting increasingly irritated by Mogoeng was evidenced when senior ANC people started briefing quietly against him in 2015. For example, at a roundtable discussion on the OCJ in spring 2015, around the time of the meeting at which Mogoeng had stood up to him and other ministers, deputy minister of justice John Jeffery sidled up to me and whispered in my ear that he had been asked to sign off on an extravagant jaunt to Australia by the chief justice. Jeffery informed me that Mogoeng not only likes to travel with a large contingent, but that he insists that his staff travel business class, while he travels first class, so that he 'is not kept waiting when he gets off the plane'. It was obvious that Jeffery hoped I would either write about it or spread the rumour, or else pass it on to the press. I did not, because the timing was obvious: it was meant to hurt Mogoeng at a particular moment in the engagement between the judiciary and the government.

Mogoeng's sense of grandeur may not be necessary or appropriate, but it may well serve to help give him the sense of power needed to withstand attacks upon his integrity and enable him to summon the resolve required to lead the judiciary. In the Nkandla judgment, in a highly charged matter of vast constitutional and political importance, the court was unanimous and so 'the Court' could have delivered the judgment, as it has on several occasions in the past. But instead, Mogoeng put his name on it. He delivered

the j
ring.
justi
furth
and
muc

have been a far stronger statement of institutional independence and intent if it had, in fact, come from 'the Court'. In a *Mail &*

Guardian interview with Niren Tolsi, Mogoeng said that he had not really had much assistance from the other nine judges in the composition of the judgment. 'There was, the truth be told, minimal input from my colleagues,' Mogoeng told Tolsi, adding that it was easy to get consensus on it: 'We had a few things to iron out, but it was not a difficult thing to get consensus on.'[13] Again, it is not easy to escape the conclusion that Mogoeng's fundamentally hubristic nature had eclipsed the need for a different kind of leadership.

Regardless of this quibble, the Nkandla judgment was forcefully delivered. And so, to answer the question posed by this chapter's subtitle: the judges can hold the line and are doing so – though as we will see in the next two chapters, much will depend on certain key appointments that will be made in the next year.

And Mogoeng, it turns out, is a chief justice *who can write.*

2

David 3, Goliath 2

How the public protector
became the people's champion

A ND WHEN MOGOENG wrote, how powerfully he did so. The Nkandla judgment delivered on 31 March 2016 was the second 'big moment' in a dramatic six-month period that changed the face – and course – of South African politics. Regardless of how it may appear right now, in time we will all come to recognise it as the period that marked the beginning of the end of the Zuma years. Or, as a long-standing Treasury source put it to me, quoting Churchill, when discussing the run-up to the extraordinarily important Budget Speech of February 2016: 'Now this is not the end. It is not even the beginning of the end. But it is, perhaps, the end of the beginning.' I thought then that my source was underestimating the speed at which events were moving back in early 2016. Zuma was

backlash against Zuma and, while being careful not to predict his immediate demise, suggested that he had to 'beware the Ides of March'. In fact, Zuma escaped being recalled by his own party at its mid-March NEC meeting, but then faced the hammer blow of the chief justice's own pen on the last day of the month, when the Constitutional Court handed down the remarkable judgment in which it held that President Zuma had violated the Constitution with regards to the Nkandla debacle.

Although the Nkandla scandal will be familiar to most if not all readers, a brief reprise of the salient factual aspects may be appropriate here. From the moment the late, brave and greatly missed young investigative journalist Mandy Rossouw broke the story in the *Mail & Guardian* in 2009, the core facts surrounding the upgrades to Zuma's private homestead at Nkandla in rural KwaZulu-Natal – for which the taxpayer would be 'footing the largest chunk of the bill', estimated to be around R246 million – have been obscured by a tissue of lies. At the outset, as Rossouw reported in that first story, the government tried to deny the allegations:

Government insisted this week that it has no record of such a development and no hand in any of Zuma's personal property endeavours.

Shortly before the *Mail & Guardian*'s deadline the presidency released a statement changing its tune. The statement reads: 'The Zuma family planned before the elections to extend the Nkandla residence, and this is being done at own cost. No government funding will be utilised for the construction work.

'Outside the perimeter of the Zuma household, a few metres from the house, the State is to undertake construction work in line with the security and medical requirements relating to

Heads of State in the Republic. The security services have to construct accommodation facilities for their staff that attend to the President, erect a helipad to ensure safe landing for the Presidential helicopter and a clinic as per medical requirements.'

Public works spokesperson Koketso Sachane said on Wednesday: 'Please note that there is no work or extension project taking place at President Jacob Zuma's homestead at Nkandla.'

The presidency also claimed no knowledge of such a project, saying that Nkandla is Zuma's private home and therefore no business of the state.

It accused the *M&G* of 'setting out to embarrass the president' by publishing a story.[1]

Around this time, I found myself engaging the Department of Public Works over an international project called the Construction Sector Transparency Initiative, a global, standard-setting initiative that seeks to ensure that key information relating to large public infrastructure projects is disclosed to the public to increase accountability and eliminate corruption. I quickly discovered that there was resistance to the idea. It was difficult to fathom, but as the Nkandla story developed, I realised why. Departmental officials were hav-

many years as a high level Committee the State Intelligence operative. It is one of subterfuge and stealth. And, more than anything, of 'plausible deniability'. Plausible deniability requires that other people do your dirty work – people like the defence officials in the case of the Waterkloof–Gupta landings, medium-level lackeys who at the end of the day are forced to carry the can. In that respect, Zuma is utterly ruthless. Unlike his predecessor, Thabo Mbeki, who rewarded loyalty, Zuma rewards it only as long as it is convenient. At the moment it becomes inconvenient, the loyalist is thrown to the lions.

But in the case of Nkandla, Zuma seems to have deviated from his usual approach. As my colleague at the University of Cape Town (UCT), Professor Pierre de Vos, so ably pointed out in his analysis of Thuli Madonsela's March 2014 report, there is ample evidence of Zuma's 'intimate involvement in (and knowledge of) the Nkandla project'. De Vos set out a sample of the numerous references to Zuma's involvement in the project in his blogged analysis.[2]

At the end of the day, the president should have known what was going on: 'As the public protector noted, any reasonable person would have seen the construction of the underground facilities and substantial landscaping interventions, the swimming pool and terrace, amphitheater, kraal and culvert, Visitors Centre, elaborate paving and the space created for a marquee tent and would have asked questions about the cost.'[3] Given Zuma's apparent knowledge of the upgrades, it is unsurprising that there is considerable disquiet about the seemingly insignificant final amount that Treasury has determined Zuma should pay (R7.8 million). Understandably, many people feel that Zuma should be carrying the can for the waste in public money. And, indeed, civil proceedings, and even corruption charges, could yet be brought against those involved, such as the president's personal architect, Minenhle Makhanya.

When Madonsela released her report in March 2014, Zuma should have simply accepted the public protector's findings and taken the remedial action that was required – namely, to pay back a proportion of the public money spent on the non-security upgrades, on the basis of a final figure to be calculated by the ministers of finance and police. Instead, Zuma obfuscated, clouding the picture by instituting competing inquiries inside government. Legally, this was a non-starter, as his legal advisors should have known and should have advised him: nothing and no one can second-guess the public protector, other than a court of law. As the Constitutional Court pointed out in its judgment, if the government could ignore Madonsela or substitute its own conclusions, then there would be little or no point in having a public protector.

The problem was that 'President Zuma' was not getting good legal advice. I use the quotation marks here deliberately. Mr Jacob Zuma, the individual, the private citizen, was getting if not good then at least convenient legal advice that served to protect or advance his interests. In other words, he was being advised first as a man, and second as a president. The reason for this is fairly straightforward. One of the two presidential legal advisors is Michael Hulley, originally Zuma's personal attorney. After his client took office in

arately and that Mr Zuma pays those invoices from his own funds. I will not hold my breath.

The point I'm trying to make with this apparently trivial but actually hugely significant matter of Zuma's attorney is that this sort of mischief permeates the whole of the Zuma presidency: there is a lack of any appreciation of the concept of conflict of interest. There is a vast and important difference between the interests of Zuma the man and Zuma the president. As Chief Justice Mogoeng put it in the Nkandla judgment: the president is a 'constitutional being by design'. In other words, the presidency is part and parcel of the Constitution. As the president, Zuma does not have his own interests, but only those of the Constitution. Hence, those who advise the president are not there to serve the interests of Zuma the man, but Zuma the constitutional being and, thereby, the interests and requirements of the Constitution. The contrast with previous presidents could not be clearer: President Mandela's legal advisor, for example, was Nicholas 'Fink' Haysom, who on several occasions was compelled to advise Mandela to do things that were no doubt uncomfortable for him and which may not have served his interests as Nelson Mandela, but which were entirely the right thing to do as president of a constitutional democracy.

In contrast, Hulley is an operator, who, as one lawyer who has dealt with him puts it, 'moves like a cat' in the shadows, loyal only to his client and master. But on Nkandla he may have made things worse. Zuma and his legal advisors thought they could get away with it. They thought they had enough power and enough yes-men and -women in government to do the necessary cover-up. They thought they could outwit the press and civil society. But they did not count on the public protector and the courts. Hulley failed to advise Zuma that while it may not have been in his interests as Jacob Zuma the individual, the right thing to do as the 'constitutional being', the president of the republic, was to accept the public protector's report and take the remedial action that was required. This is how the conflict of interest at the heart of the presidency serves to corrupt the public interest and the Constitution.

The Constitutional Court dissected the president's failure to uphold the Constitution in a deliberately straightforward and accessible judgment. When Mogoeng was appointed chief justice, one of the concerns that many of us had was that he would allow his devout Christianity to trump constitutional values. In the Nkandla judgment, the biblical rhetorical flourish that he employed to make his point provided appropriately accessible and striking imagery: '[The public protector] is the embodiment of a biblical David, that the public is, who fights the most powerful and very well-resourced Goliath, that impropriety and corruption by government officials are.'[4]

This, then, is the role of the public protector: to be David to government's Goliath. And how well has Madonsela played the role! She has been a thorn in the government's side since her appointment in mid-2009. So how on earth did Thuli Madonsela end up as public protector? This is a question I have been asked many times over the past few years. Like many such things, it is not entirely clear

around half the board of the South African Broadcasting Corporation (SABC); a couple of human rights commissioners, including

41

a new chair; and a new public protector. If memory serves, it all happened in a week or two in August 2009. The ANC's attention was on the SABC board, as was the media's. There was some real controversy there. In terms of 'state capture', Zuma's securocrats had greater control of the state broadcaster at the top of their list. The South African Human Rights Commission (SAHRC) and the Office of the Public Protector were deemed to be not as important. Neither had been making many waves in recent years. Advocate Lawrence Mushwana had proved to be a 'sweetheart' public protector, rarely troubling the executive and shying away from anything remotely difficult or controversial. The low point of his seven-year term as public protector was his refusal to 'follow the money' in the notorious 'Oilgate' scandal, when R11 million of public money was siphoned off to the ANC via PetroSA, a failure by the public protector that the Supreme Court of Appeal later slammed.[5] Mushwana was duly rewarded by not only being given one of the vacant SAHRC positions, but also being chosen to chair the commission. From public protector to chair of the Human Rights Commission: rarely in the history of human endeavour has such insipid mediocrity achieved back-to-back appointments to such high constitutional offices.

I remember attending the hearings for the SAHRC vacancies. Hardly anyone was watching. Likewise with the public protector. Although South Africa's much-vaunted 'civil society' is rich in talent, it also has blind spots, as were exposed that week. Luckily for everyone, there were others with blind spots. The then dean of the UCT law school, P.J. Schwikkard, informed me that having served with Madonsela on the Law Reform Commission, she could report that Madonsela was nothing special and we should prepare to be disappointed. How wrong she proved to be. Madonsela is in many ways the ideal character to serve as an ombud, which is the primary role of the constitutional body created as one of the six 'chapter nine' institutions supporting constitutional democracy (named after Chapter 9 of the Constitution). Fighting corruption, taking on the vested interests that often lie behind maladministration, requires a special personality. Madonsela has it. She is strong-willed, independent-minded, obdurate to the point of stubbornness, rather arrogant and certainly thick-skinned. And, above all, probably a tad eccentric. In the same way that they say most goalkeepers are a bit mad, so, I suspect, most (good) ombuds are also a minister of finance short of a full cabinet. In other words, you have to be a bit bonkers to do the job properly.

With all due respect to Madonsela – and I have a lot of respect for her and how she has withstood a great deal of intimidation in recent years from some heavyweight people within government and the ruling party – you have to enjoy the limelight, as Madonsela clearly does. You have to relish the fight, and you have to be willing to give as good as you get. You can't be a shrinking violet. If anything, at times Madonsela has gone too far in this respect. She would, for example, have been wisely advised to keep well away from her Twitter account. Some of her tweets have not been appro-

period of Kgalema Motlanthe's caretaker administration, created opportunity for appointments such as Madonsela's and that of Edwin Cameron, the activist human rights lawyer who Motlanthe appointed to the Constitutional Court in late 2008 – neither Mbeki nor Zuma would have made such a brave (and correct) appointment to the court. My expectation, and hope, is that South Africa is entering a similar period now; that as Zuma's power wanes and a different sort of transition begins, with a variety of competing forces and impulses, so again we will see a loosening of control on events and processes and institutions.

The process of choosing Madonsela's successor for when her term expires in October 2016 will be a test of this proposition. Clearly, this time it will get plenty of attention, from the ANC and from civil society. Already there is a 'Bua Mzansi' (Speak up, South Africa) campaign, led by Corruption Watch, to monitor the process and to ensure that it is not hijacked by the control freaks in the ruling party who may well be anxious to avoid a repeat of the Madonsela 'mistake'.[6] One obvious candidate is Madonsela's current deputy, Advocate Kevin Sifiso Malunga. Although he may contest this, the sagacity and judgement necessary for an ombud come at least partly with age and experience, and Malunga may be a bit on the young side. Yet there is no doubting his talent or his ambition. He is a very impressive individual, who certainly has the swagger that may be a prerequisite for the office. For a rather awkward period in mid-2013, Malunga seemed to have deserted his boss. They appeared to be at loggerheads, privately briefing against each other. It suggested that Malunga may have been trying to signal to the ANC leadership that there was clear blue water between him and Madonsela and that they should not be 'tarred with the same brush'. As the public took Madonsela's side over Nkandla and she became a darling not just of the chattering classes but across the republic,[7] it seems that Malunga shifted his position, smart enough to recognise on which side of history one should be seen to end up. Attributing such an opportunistic approach to Malunga may not be fair to him. Certainly, I am willing to stick to my first instinctive impression of him, which is one of a man of calibre and integrity. Indeed, it may be that in 2013 he was simply expressing justified caution towards some of the more flamboyant public poses that Madonsela was striking.

Speaking of which, given what she went through, only the most churlish would have objected to Madonsela's real moment in the sun, when, in a dramatic, canary-yellow gown, she walked up Government Avenue at the February 2016 state opening of Parliament. Halfway up the red carpet, guests and MPs are supposed to pause for a moment or two so that the bank of waiting photojournalists can take pictures. Madonsela 'paused' for at least twenty minutes. She was basking in the praise that was understandably being heaped upon her. My former colleague at the Institute for Democracy in Africa, Moira Levy, who now works for Parliament's media department and has herself been courageous enough to blow the whistle on dodgy goings-on among the senior management of Parliament, and who is as prone to cynicism as any other old hand of journo,

pendence of the Constitutional Court.

Who succeeds Madonsela, and how and on what basis that decision is taken, is important not only because it is one of the big six signposts along the crucial road of the next three years – vital because of the public protector's role in fighting corruption in government – but also in terms of what it tells us about the balance of forces within the ANC's leadership and their attitude to constitutional democracy and key institutions, such as the judiciary and the public protector. In this respect, the ANC has flip-flopped intriguingly over the past twelve months – from the bullying bravado of its attacks on Madonsela in 2015 and its full-on engagement with the judiciary, all guns blazing, to the statement issued by Luthuli House on the day of the Constitutional Court hearing on the Nkandla matter on 9 February 2016. That statement professed a commitment to constitutional institutions that had been conspicuous by its absence in the previous year. There was also the respect accorded to Madonsela by ANC MPs when, exactly a week after the Nkandla judgment, she appeared before the parliamentary justice committee to deliver her annual budget. In recent years this had been an occasion of great animosity. ANC MPs have used it to get stuck into Madonsela; in 2013, it was the time when the division between Malunga and his boss seemed most obvious and concerning. But on Thursday 7 April 2016, the mood was entirely different, as ANC MP after ANC MP took it upon themselves to greet Madonsela and attempt to bury the hatchet (though it is also true that two weeks after that they were refusing to apologise formally to her).

Why the about-turn? Well, even bad politicians can detect when they are losing. Besides, their president had essentially capitulated to Madonsela at the eleventh hour. Dramatically, at the Nkandla hearing on 9 February, Zuma's counsel had conceded that, in fact, his client *did* accept that the public protector's powers were binding. This was an extraordinary U-turn. There were gasps from the public gallery in the Constitutional Court. The mood was similar to that in 2002 when the court heard another landmark case: the Treatment Action Campaign application for a declaratory order that the Mbeki administration's refusal to provide access to nevirapine, a drug that evidence suggested had a 70 per cent chance of preventing mother-to-child transmission of HIV, was a violation of the Constitution. Judges are not immune to what is going on around them. They can smell the zeitgeist. Just as in 2002 the mood in the country was one of anger and frustration with Mbeki's quixotic intransigence in the face of an obvious health crisis, so too in 2016 the court could no doubt sense that the country was *gatvol* of Zuma's implausible attempts to deny responsibility to 'pay back the money' – the typically punchy slogan that Julius Malema and his red-overalled EFF MPs had adopted in Parliament throughout 2015, as they repeatedly disrupted parliamentary proceedings and made life uncomfortable for Zuma.

What had made Zuma do his U-turn? The short answer: his legal counsel, the identity of whom was entirely surprising. In late 2015, Zuma had retained Jeremy Gauntlett SC, a doyen of constitutional law but hardly a darling of the ANC. Indeed, the ANC representatives on the JSC had on no fewer than five occasions blocked Gauntlett's candidature for judicial appointment. They regarded him as far too arrogant, independent-minded and DA-aligned. Arguably, it is a sign of just how desperate Zuma and his legal team were that they decided to turn to Gauntlett, who was astonished to receive a call from Hulley in late 2015. The penny must have dropped with Hulley that the stakes were now very high and that his principal needed to hear from a fresh legal source.

Unable to resist the obvious allure of such a big-ticket brief, Gauntlett decided to allow this surprising turn of events to interrupt his usually sacrosanct end-of-year holiday. Between Christmas and New Year Gauntlett sat on the deck of his home in Simon's Town and read the Nkandla papers. It is clear that Gauntlett advised Zuma not only that the legal position was straightforward – that the public protector's directive to 'take remedial action' is binding unless challenged by way of judicial review – but also that the stance the president had taken both in his legal papers and in Parliament would be found to be in violation of the Constitution. The only question, Gauntlett must have advised Zuma, was how the court would frame its judgment. Would they go as far as laying the ground for impeachment?

The 'I word' thus raised its head, though unlike in Brazil and the United States there is no such process available in the South African system. Although the Constitution does not use the word, section 89 in effect provides for Parliament itself to remove a sitting president when he has committed a 'serious violation of the Constitution'. None of the parties to the Nkandla matter were pushing for 'impeachment'. They simply wanted to confirm the powers of the public protector and secure a declarator from the court that the president and Parliament had violated the Constitution in failing to 'defend, uphold and respect' it by refusing to take the public protector's remedial action. It was Gauntlett, not Wim Trengove SC as counsel for the EFF or Anton Katz SC for the DA, who brought 'impeachment' into play during the hearing.

On the one hand, it made Zuma look weaker: he was accepting that he was on thin ice and needed to concede crucial, fundamental ground in order to avoid the ultimate fate. On the other hand, it may have been a brilliant, as well as necessary, tactical move designed to take the heat out of the judgment. My hunch is that Gauntlett, knowing full well that he would never again find himself representing Zuma, and probably entirely indifferent to that fact, took it upon himself to take his instructions to their furthest limit. I know from my own career as a barrister (advocate) at the London Bar before coming to South Africa in 1994 that there are occasions when your client provides you with instructions that give you a large amount of latitude. If you are so inclined, you can manipulate the situation a little, to increase that latitude to its fullest – sometimes for very good reason and not gratuitously – so as to give maximum tactical flexibility to one's submissions in court, for example. Whether consciously or subconsciously, Gauntlett may have seen it as his professional duty, to the court and to the Constitution, to advise his client in the way that he did and to create the space to legitimately and justifiably make the dramatic, game-changing concessions that he did in court on behalf of Zuma. It may have saved the president's bacon or it may have made things a bit worse. Whichever it was, Zuma finally had a lawyer who was advising him as the president and not as a private citizen. As a result, the interests of the presidency, and the Constitution, were served. But not necessarily those of Mr Jacob Zuma, who was pushed one big step further towards his political downfall.

3

Appointing judges, Malema-style

The Constitutional Court
and the importance of the JSC

A FEW DAYS BEFORE the seminal and, for Jacob Zuma, devastating Constitutional Court judgment in the Nkandla case, Public Protector Thuli Madonsela went to see Zuma, a fact that I believe is not widely known. It was a strange thing to do, perhaps in keeping with Madonsela's eccentricity and her willingness, like Frank Sinatra, to do it her way. It may be that it accorded with some notion of cultural respect or served to indicate that whatever the outcome, it was not personal, that she had simply been doing her job. Or perhaps she was trying to take care of her future career after she ceases to be public protector in October 2016, though it is hard to imagine that she will be short of offers from a variety of domestic and international sources.

Madonsela has done an extraordinarily important job as public protector and will be very difficult to replace. As noted in the previous chapter, the question of who replaces her is one of the significant signposts for the future. But hers is not the only important vacancy to be filled. Up to now I have offered an essentially positive perspective on the state of important institutions in South Africa, such as the public protector and the higher courts.

However, I also recognise that some others, particularly those in the criminal justice sphere, such as the National Prosecuting Authority (NPA), are not in a good state and have been intentionally vandalised. As of July 2016, two positions had become vacant on the Constitutional Court: Justice Johann van der Westhuizen completed his term in early 2016, and Deputy Chief Justice Dikgang Moseneke served his last day on the bench on Friday 20 May 2016 (even though his term does not formally come to an end until October, he has taken leave that was owed to him).

Van der Westhuizen and Moseneke's departures represent the third significant moment for the Constitutional Court since 2009, when four leading intellectual lights of the court completed their terms at the same time. Justices Pius Langa, Albie Sachs, Yvonne Mokgoro and Kate O'Regan, who had all served the court since its establishment in 1996, constituted what was widely regarded by legal academics as the court's 'progressive wing'. Their departure was a huge moment for the court and its ideological and jurisprudential make-up. Among the four appointments to replace the renowned group was – to the great surprise of almost everyone – Mogoeng Mogoeng. Even fewer would have predicted that just two years later, in 2011, he would become chief justice, replacing Sandile Ngcobo, in the second significant moment in the court's development in recent years.

By the end of 2016, in addition to the 'big four' juristic luminaries who departed in 2009, the Constitutional Court will have lost three more of its progressive members: namely, Ngcobo, architect of many of the court's most far-reaching, pro-human-rights judgments of the last decade and a half; Van der Westhuizen, who usually sided with the likes of Ngcobo, O'Regan and Moseneke; and Moseneke, who, aside from his abilities as a lawyer, has a CV that perhaps only Cyril Ramaphosa can match in terms of variety of extraordinarily significant leadership positions. Imprisoned on Robben Island when he was just fifteen for ten long years, Moseneke has suffered great personal loss. As he said to the judicial forum convened by the Democratic Governance and Rights Unit (DGRU) at Mont Fleur in November 2015, 'I got on that boat to Robben Island as virgin. Imagine what it was like for a fifteen-year-old to be sent there at that age.'

Moseneke was a giant of a judge and is a giant of a human being. He showed remarkable resolve in remaining on the court and not throwing his toys out of the cot when he was overlooked not once but twice to be chief justice, simply because the ANC and Zuma were too small-minded and parochial to see past the judge's own independence of mind.

For anyone having watched Moseneke destroy Mogoeng during the latter's interview by the Judicial Service Commission in September 2011, and having seen the obvious enmity between the two men, it is hard to believe that they forged a strong working relationship. It was not plain sailing. But Moseneke's role as deputy was crucial in ensuring that Mogoeng's lack of experience in running a big court (he came from being judge president of the smallest High Court division in the land) and his lack of jurisprudential clout did not seriously diminish the court's ability to operate effectively. At times, however, it was not possible to paper over the cracks. I have mentioned Mogoeng's managerial failure in permitting a situation whereby four acting justices served on the court in the first half of 2015. There is already a substantive problem with acting appointments, in that while permanent appointments to the bench go through the elaborate and transparent process of the JSC and its public interviews, acting appointments are made secretly, at the discretion of the judge presidents of the courts, with the minister of justice just signing off.

Moseneke and several of his colleagues were not happy with the fact that the Constitutional Court had four acting judges; it added to their workload and pressure, having so many novices acting on the court. I raise a different objection, one that concerns the effect on the independence of the court, or the perception of independence. Acting judges are, by definition, 'trying out' for the job. In most cases they are hoping for an appointment. They want and need to do well. Their performance when acting will invariably come up when they are interviewed by the JSC. And given the way in which the JSC has often approached issues of separation of powers in recent years, an acting judge might be forgiven if he or she were a little less robust in their approach to adjudication than if they were fully appointed. I am not suggesting that there would be an overt attempt to 'suck up' to the government, although it is possible, but rather that subconsciously it might affect the individual's approach to a 'hard' political case.

Certainly, having four acting appointees on the bench at the same time struck us at the DGRU as imprudent, and so I wrote, in what I thought were polite and diplomatic terms, to Chief Justice Mogoeng saying as much. That was on 27 March 2015. There was no immediate reply, but on Sunday 12 April, at precisely 20:35, a 2 200-word emailed reply plopped into my inbox. Although I chose not to publicise my letter, and it was not cc'd to anyone else, the chief justice's reply was copied to the minister of justice as well as some officials. It accused me of suggesting that the acting judges were corrupt, in the following terms:

One of the key concerns you raise is that acting appointments are undesirable because acting Judges are likely to bow down to illegitimate pressure and make or align themselves with decisions that are in favour of the appointing authorities. They could, in your view, also do so of their own accord in order to brighten their prospects of securing permanent appointment. This you say is likely to happen when people are acting in the apex court. In my book, only a Head of Court or a Judge who is corrupt will behave in the manner alluded to in your letter. If these assertions are correct, they must apply not only to those acting in the apex court but also to those acting in all other courts. Meaning, every Advocate and every Attorney who is acting as a High Court Judge and desires permanent appointment, is likely to either succumb to pressure or choose to act in a corrupt way by taking decisions in a manner intended to endear themselves to the appointing authority. What lies at the heart of the decision to disregard the affirmation or oath of office, the rules of ethics and the Constitution, is not the court one wishes to be appointed to. It is rather the desperation to be appointed permanently. That is why I say, this premise applies to anyone who has acted or will act as a Judge and wished or wishes to be appointed permanently. Given the seriousness and far-reaching implications of your comments, it would have been helpful to substantiate them.

But there was nothing to substantiate, since I was not accusing the four acting judges of corruption or any other kind of impropriety. What I was suggesting was that having four acting judges out of eleven was unwise, since it might create a perception in a politically charged case, with a split court, that those seeking permanent appointment had swung the decision in favour of the government or some other political interest group.

As it turned out, one such case came along almost immediately: *My Vote Counts NPC v Speaker of the National Assembly and Others*.[1] Heard on 10 February 2015, when four acting judges were on the court, it was a case that went right to the heart of the political economy of the country – who funds political parties, and especially the ANC – and divided the Constitutional Court. Its 30 September 2015 judgment dismissing the application split the court 7-4. At issue was whether Parliament was under a constitutional duty to introduce legislation to regulate private funding of political parties. At present, there is no regulation, and dodgy donors can exert influence in secret by making donations of any size without any duty to disclose to anyone. It is a massive, gaping lacuna, from which many of the corruption scandals of the last twenty years, including the arms deal and most likely now the nuclear deal, have stemmed. It is difficult to think of a case with greater political sensitivity, as well as serious separation-of-powers issues, because if the minority of four judges had prevailed, Parliament would have been found to have been in violation of the Constitution in not passing a transparency law and would probably have been required to do so, by order of the court. The majority judgment found that there was no such duty, and that the applicants should have attacked the Promotion of Access to Information Act for its failure to properly encompass records of private donations. The majority judgment was written by four judges and supported by three. Of the seven, three were acting judges. One acting judge, Judge Achmat Jappie, concurred with the minority judgment written by Justice Edwin

Cameron, along with justices Moseneke and Johan Froneman. Clearly, the three acting judges on the majority side could have swung the mathematics in favour of the applicants. And, as a result, there were more than just murmurings of discontent at the outcome of the case from the applicants, the transparency pressure group My Vote Counts.

I should add that none of the four acting judges has subsequently been appointed to the Constitutional Court. Since then, only one appointment has been made, and that was Nonkosi Mhlantla in November 2015.

But I am ruminating, to use one of Moseneke's favourite words. The question now is, who will replace Moseneke, both as a member of the Constitutional Court and as deputy chief justice? It matters a great deal, especially because President Zuma has far more power when appointing the deputy chief justice (as well as the chief justice and the president and deputy president of the Supreme Court of Appeal). In the case of the chief and deputy chief justices, Zuma appoints after simply 'consulting' (a relatively low-level requirement that is easy to discharge) the JSC and the leaders of the parties represented in the National Assembly, whereas for all other High Court, Constitutional Court and SCA appointments, the JSC has the biggest hand in that the president must appoint 'on the advice of' the JSC, meaning that he has very little room to manoeuvre. Hence it is possible that Zuma could helicopter someone in from left field, as it were, to take over the deputy chief justice position, someone whom he thinks will be more sympathetic to his cause and more docile in relation to government violations of the Constitution. If so, it will be interesting to see how the JSC handles its role. Since the deputy chief justice must also be a member of the Constitutional Court, it is difficult to imagine that the constitution-makers intended such an outside appointment to escape the rigour of the appointment process for an 'ordinary' Constitutional Court judge. We shall have to wait and see.

As the *My Vote Counts* judgment illustrated, the court is more divided than ever before. Or, rather, it appears more stubbornly divided along ideological or jurisprudential philosophical lines than during the days of the 'first court' from 1996 to 2009. Interestingly, although there are now judges who are widely regarded as 'conservative' or legal 'formalists' – principally, justices Chris Jafta and Ray Zondo, described to me as 'aggressively conservative' by one fellow member of the judiciary – since the progressive wing of the court has held a majority, the court has tended to be more assertive and creative than the old first court, perhaps because the chief justice's ability to forge consensus, and thereby compromise, no longer exists. The progressive end of the court has been liberated to be more adventurous.

That progressive wing has comprised, broadly speaking, Deputy Chief Justice Moseneke and justices Cameron and Froneman, with Justice Van der Westhuizen generally aligned, and Mbuyiseli Madlanga sometimes joining this (tepidly) 'left' grouping. Mogoeng and Bess Nkabinde tend, with some exceptions, to instinctively side with the more conservative grouping. Sisi Khampepe and Mhlantla are, more or less, either more conservatively inclined or swing voters in the middle, and are often heavily influenced by Moseneke (his 'jurisprudential leadership will, thus, leave a big hole', in the view of one judge). These, I must hasten to add, are broad brushstrokes; the scope of this book does not permit a more careful or academically sound exposition on the political contours of the court.

But clearly, the political equilibrium of the court is in the balance: the next two appointments could shift it away from its current broadly progressive bent. That is why rumours that Edwin Cameron might retire earlier than his due date in 2021 have caused such concern in some quarters. Which brings us to the Judicial Service Commission, an important institutional creature whose significance and influence on political events is only just becoming more widely understood. This is partly because of the assiduousness of a small group of reporters – Niren Tolsi and Franny Rabkin especially – and the hard work of my colleagues at the DGRU, particularly Chris Oxtoby and Tabeth Masengu, but also because of the relatively new campaign group Judges Matter, led by the irrepressible and astute veteran human rights activist Alison Tilley. Working together, the DGRU and its research reports, and the social media exuberance of Judges Matter, including live streaming of the last set of interviews in April 2016, have brought the JSC to the attention of a much bigger group of people. But there is another factor: Julius Malema. The EFF leader now serves on the JSC.

The JSC is an unusual, hybrid structure, comprising eleven politicians – six MPs from the National Assembly, four members from the National Council of Provinces and the minister of justice – plus eight judges and lawyers, and four people nominated by the president, who actually makes the final appointments, usually 'on the advice of' the JSC. As an example of the constitution-makers' understanding of the importance of judicial appointments and the need for legitimacy, they inserted a modest yet notable constitutional provision that is a neat example of the notion of counter-majoritarianism at work: regardless of the size of the majority of the ruling party, at least three – i.e. 50 per cent – of the six MPs on the JSC must be from opposition parties. This is an important institutional safeguard. And while it is true that on the current numbers it is possible for the ANC to secure the majority of twelve it needs to push through its candidate for judicial appointment if the four presidential nominees are willing to act in a partisan fashion, I believe that by and large the JSC has not succumbed to one-party dominance and is doing a good job, albeit with occasional appalling procedural lapses (such as the one concerning Judge Clive Plasket that I detailed in *The Zuma Years*[2]). Moreover, since 2014, the ANC members of the JSC have greatly elevated the tone and content of the questions. Instead of obsessing over separation of powers as Fatima Chohan did, Thoko Didiza and Thandi Modise in particular have focused on issues of gender equality and human rights, as well as the jurisprudential outlook of the candidate. The trend is in the right direction. And, while it can be a terrifying experience even for experienced judges to appear before the JSC, it is an institution that one can put in the plus column when assessing the quality of South African constitutional democracy and institutional infrastructure.

Part of why appearing before the JSC can be terrifying is the directness of the questions, especially from one Honourable Malema. When Judge Rosheni Allie was being grilled in April 2016 about a highly regrettable series of WhatsApp messages that she had exchanged with Professor Ziyad Motala, which denigrated not just some of her colleagues on the Western Cape High Court but also the chief justice, who recused himself and watched the unfolding train wreck of an interview on the DGRU live stream, it was Malema who stuck in the knife with a simple bit of cross-examination: 'Do you agree that judges should be honourable?' Yes. 'Do you agree that you have behaved dishonourably?' No. 'But you have. You are not an honourable person. You are not fit to be a judge, are you?'

In another life, Malema ought to be an advocate. He would be hugely effective. When Chris Oxtoby discovered that the EFF had decided to take up one of the three places available to the opposition, he excitedly sent me a text message with the news that Malema would be on the JSC. 'Good,' was my simple reply. I knew that Malema would not only be an effective member of the commission because he has everything to gain from an independent bench, but would also be able to join the dots and ensure that any political bullying in the JSC would cost the ANC outside of its quiet proceedings. That is what Malema does best: join the dots and cause the ANC problems. He knows how to hurt them. He knows how to turn big, complex issues into sharp sound bites. And he is dexterous, as his performance on the JSC shows. He can, to use a political campaigning term, bifurcate. One day he is the anti-establishment hero, standing up to the political elite in revolutionary style and apparel in Parliament, disrupting proceedings and encouraging violence and institutional disarray. The next he is standing in front of the Constitutional Court speaking eloquently about the importance of the rule of law and democratic institutions. Then, he will turn up to the JSC in a dark suit but with a bright-red tie – to sustain the branding – and ask crisp, focused questions that show his understanding both of his role as a commissioner and of what is needed in a good judge.

What a bundle of contradictions. What an interesting fellow. He has breathed life into important yet atrophying parts of South Africa's political system and shown how a complacent and decadent ANC can be discomforted. Yet Malema is also dangerous because he is unprincipled. His charisma and sharp mind, and equally sharply defined political brand, mean that he is a real threat to the ruling party. But can he turn these political attributes into votes?

4

Game changer

The 2016 local government elections

IN THE AUGUST 2016 local government elections, the ANC
faced a serious threat to its political hegemony for the first
time since it came to power in 1994. Driving around Soweto and
Alexandria on election day, Wednesday 3 August, there was little to
suggest that it would be anything other than business-as-usual, with
no real indication of the drama that was to unfold over the coming
thirty-six hours. People like me love election night but are bored
by election day itself. Nothing really happens. People arrive and
stand in line and vote. There might be the odd incident or two –
happily very little of any great concern or import occurred on
3 August – but campaigning is limited to trying to get out the vote
and media is similarly constrained by law to report on the facts of
the electoral process rather than the campaigns and issues. It is
a frustrating pause before the real action starts once the polls have
closed. But even then, results trickle in painfully slowly. It was only
as dawn broke on 4 August that the results of the first of about
thirty 'bellwether' wards and voting districts that I had identified
as key started to come in. At 7:55 a.m. I decided it was safe to stick
my social-media neck out, so to speak, and tweet: 'ANC taking some
significant hits in working class areas in TSH & NMB. Could lose
both. Coalition time!'

I was not surprised. I had been living in anticipation of this for some time, predicting to all and sundry that this would be a game-changing election. In an earlier draft of this chapter, I wrote: 'The extraordinary thing is this: despite its ostensibly decisive victory in 2014 in the national election, the ANC could wake up on 4 August 2016 and find that it has a majority (i.e. more than 50 per cent of the council seats) in only *one* of the five big metros. For the ANC to have less than 50 per cent of the council seats in Johannesburg, Cape Town, Pretoria and Port Elizabeth would be a huge jolt to the party and a massive psychological shock. Were the ANC to fall beneath 50 per cent in just Port Elizabeth, it would be a significant result. To do so in Pretoria and/or Johannesburg, would be a huge result, and a big game changer for South African politics.'

And so it turned out. As the table on the following page sets out, the ANC suffered significant losses in Tshwane (Pretoria), Johannesburg and Nelson Mandela Bay (Port Elizabeth), dropping to well below 50 per cent of the votes and council seats (seats are allocated on the basis of wards won and votes on a proportional representation, or PR, party list system) in all three of these key battlegrounds – a huge psychological blow for the ruling party and an enormous boost for the opposition.

Why was I able to make these predictions? The 2014 national election result contained contradictory messages. On the one hand, it was a decisive victory for the ANC: anything over 60 per cent is always, by definition, a clear win. And in five national elections since 1994, the ANC has never got less than 62 per cent of the popular vote. That is impressive. The ANC is a robust political animal with a strong capacity for mobilising its vote when it matters

PARTY	%	SEATS
Tshwane		
ANC	41 (-14)	89 (-29)
DA	43 (+8)	93 (+11)
EFF	10 (+10)	25 (+25)
Johannesburg		
ANC	45 (-14)	121 (-32)
DA	38 (+3)	104 (+14)
EFF	11 (+11)	30 (+30)
Nelson Mandela Bay		
ANC	41 (-9)	50 (-13)
DA	47 (+7)	57 (+9)
EFF	5 (+5)	6 (+6)

© 'What now? South Africa's 2016 local government elections', report by
The Paternoster Group, August 2016. Written and edited by Richard Calland,
Ian Farmer and Lawson Naidoo, with Nathan Dufour as lead researcher.

most. And, of course, it has a very powerful political brand, based
on a particular, long history and the so-called democracy dividend
that comes from having been the party of liberation. On the other
hand, the ANC's victory was less than convincing in some key areas.
For example, in Gauteng – the economic heart of the country –
the party barely hung on to its majority, dropping 17 percentage
points in ten years, from a commanding 70 per cent in 2004 to
53 per cent in 2014. Gauteng is the province with two of the five
biggest metropolitan governments or 'metros': Tshwane and Johannesburg. The other three are Cape Town, Durban and Nelson
Mandela Bay. And although the ANC dropped just 1.6 percentage
points to 48.5 per cent in Nelson Mandela Bay when compared with
the previous 2009 national election, the DA grew its support there

by almost 13 percentage points to 41 per cent in the same period. The evidence of electoral decline was therefore already apparent, especially in the urban areas which would be the key battlegrounds for the 2016 municipal elections.

The big questions that have hung over South African politics for the last twenty years are these: What happens when the ANC's liberation brand starts to wane? Will it, in fact, ever wane, or can it be sustained indefinitely? And, an inevitable corollary, how will the so-called born-free generation vote?

Taking the corollary question first, there are again contradictory messages. The born-frees seem simultaneously to be more politically active and less so, and the difference between the two appears to have a lot to do with class. The student protest movement of 2015 – in itself a game-changing political event – suggested that those born-frees with the means and access to resources such as social media and knowledge and networks could mobilise powerfully. Yet the evidence from 2014 was that a worryingly large proportion of the six million people who were entitled to vote but did not even register to do so were the working-class members of society under thirty years of age. This number is concerning because it suggests that these young people are dropping out of politics and the democratic system, presumably because they see no real point in participating in electoral processes. The 2016 local government elections were, therefore, also an important gauge of whether representative democracy in South Africa is in crisis or whether it still enjoys legitimacy. While turnout on election day was steady – an almost identical figure to 2011 of around 58 per cent – a similar proportion of the eligible voting population again failed to register.

As to the questions concerning the ANC and the enduring strength of its political brand, the party went into the 2016 elections significantly weakened. I have identified several possible reasons why this may be so, the first of which is that the party is finding it increasingly difficult to raise the big bucks it needs to fund its massive political machine. Many of the people who used to happily write out cheques for the ANC are no longer willing to do so. Indeed, many of the ANC-aligned black businessmen would be glad to see the ANC suffer a little at the polls because they hope it will provoke the party to get rid of the man they detest: Jacob Zuma. I am talking here about, for example, the Patrice Motsepes of this world and other members of the wealthy black elite – grand associates of the ANC's traditional business and politics embrace, not the arriviste members of the Zumaist crony political economy, represented most obviously by the Gupta family (though one should not forget that the Guptas' relationship with the ANC pre-dates Zuma). Notwithstanding these sentiments, money did not seem to be a particular problem for the ANC in 2016. On the contrary, there was ample evidence of a no-expense-spared campaign, with all the usual trappings, from thousands of free T-shirts at rallies and vast banner adverts in airports and alongside freeways to VIP helicopters for mayoral candidates. The head of the ANC's campaign, Nomvula Mokonyane, at one point let slip that the party had spent a record R1 billion (although ANC treasurer Zweli Mkhize later refused to confirm the figure or provide an alternative).

The second possible reason is that the ANC no longer has such a big COSATU organisational machine to help it run a massive campaign. COSATU is smaller and less powerful than it was.

Important members of the union federation, such as the National Union of Metalworkers of South Africa (NUMSA), have left. In Nelson Mandela Bay, for example, the United Front established by NUMSA and former COSATU general secretary Zwelinzima Vavi may have ended up with only 1 per cent of the vote overall, but in some working-class areas harvested around 6 per cent, almost certainly entirely from the ANC.

Third, the electorate is getting younger, and younger voters are less loyal to the ANC. Trends noted by the Afrobarometer series have tracked how party identity has persistently fallen over the years: the younger you are, the less likely you are to identify with the ANC. And 'identification', rather than who you will vote for tomorrow, is taken by pollsters as a far more important underlying trend.

Fourth, local government elections tend to yield lower turnouts than national elections (2016 was good, at around 58 per cent, an almost identical figure to 2011, but still lower than the 2014 national election, which saw over 70 per cent). Lower turnouts tend to favour opposition parties who are pushing for change rather than incumbent ruling parties who are typically suffering from a mid-term dip in popularity. And in August 2016, this effect was 'differentiated' in that there was a striking contrast between suburban areas, where the opposition were stronger and where turnout was far higher, and working-class township areas, where there was a comparatively lower turnout as ANC voters stayed away from the polls, prompting Gwede Mantashe to say, 'Black people don't appreciate the value of voting.' While the ANC's failure to 'get out their vote' is a negative for the party, as it is clear evidence of a protest vote against them, they will draw some comfort from the fact that the core stay-away voters did not transfer their vote to other parties. This will encourage the ANC to think that they can reclaim their support in 2019.

Fifth, the general sense of unease about the economy and future prospects ate away at ANC voters' confidence in 'their' party, an effect that was particularly marked in cities, because, as 2014 showed quite clearly, there is an emerging trend in which ANC support is stronger and more loyal in the rural areas or smaller provinces than in the big cities (and their provinces). As a result, it was not hard to predict that the ANC would likely be hit hardest in Pretoria and Johannesburg, where, in addition, the DA and the EFF invested most of their own campaign resources.

That factor is the sixth: the opposition are stronger than before and able to capitalise on ANC weaknesses. The minnow parties have been squeezed, so the non-ANC vote is no longer too thinly spread – although in August 2016 the Inkatha Freedom Party (IFP) bounced back a little from the edge of its political grave.

Seventh and lastly, the ANC has a leader who has gone from being an electoral asset to an electoral liability. In the last two national elections, Zuma was hugely valuable to the ANC because of his popularity in his home province of KwaZulu-Natal. In 2009 the ANC went down 8 per cent on average in eight of the nine provinces, but in KwaZulu-Natal it went up 16 per cent, meaning that it fell by only 4 per cent overall – part of the 'big bucket' syndrome of national elections in South Africa. In early 2016, however, Afrobarometer data revealed that Zuma's popularity had fallen significantly across race and class groups across the country. Their May 2016 report stated: 'The proportion of South Africans who say they trust the president "somewhat" or "a lot" dropped by almost half between 2011 and 2015, from 62% to 34%, reaching its second-lowest level since the first Afrobarometer survey in 2000. Among 11 countries surveyed in Southern Africa, Zuma has the second-lowest level of public trust, higher only than Malawi's ex-President Joyce Banda.'[1]

In Gauteng, where the ANC provincial executive committee called for him to step down, Zuma is especially unpopular. And in Port Elizabeth, in the Eastern Cape, where Zuma's Zulu ethnicity is a disadvantage, he was unlikely to do the ANC much good – hence the DA's smart campaign billboard in which they declared that ANC mayoral candidate Danny Jordaan had been 'Proudly brought to you by Jacob Zuma'.

It was therefore inevitable that the 2016 local government elections would be a referendum on Zuma. He will no doubt deny this, and so the question is whether his organisation remains in denial or moves beyond it and recognises what needs to be done if it is to recover its political savoir-faire. Aside from the potential impact of the result on Zuma's hold on power within the ANC, there were three other critical questions going into the 2016 elections:

1. Would the ANC black working-class vote hold up in the three key battlegrounds of Nelson Mandela Bay, Tshwane and Johannesburg?
2. Has the DA made any inroads in those areas to suggest that it can break through the proverbial 'glass ceiling' that limits its prospects of offering a credible alternative to the ANC at national level?
3. Would the EFF build on its 2014 performance?

As dawn broke on 4 August and the first significant urban results came in, it rapidly became clear that the ANC was getting a bloody nose in areas where normally it does very well, specifically township areas. Black working-class voters, it seemed, were offering the ANC a remarkable, sharp rebuke. I pored over the excellent IEC website, looking for results from a 'hit list' of around thirty bellwether wards. In Tshwane, I was on the lookout for those areas where intra-party conflict and violence erupted when the ANC made such a hash of choosing its mayoral candidate for the city in June, just two months before election day. I was not disappointed in my expectation that there might be some kind of correlation between the evidence of disaffection in June and the results in August. In Ward 21 in Mabopane, for example, the final results showed that ANC support fell dramatically from 83 per cent at the last municipal elections in 2011 to 59 per cent now, with the DA's vote doubling to about 19 per cent and the EFF harvesting a similar score. But the DA's high score here seemed to be an exception to the rule in these working-class areas. Although a similar drop in ANC support was observed in Ward 15 in Mamelodi, here it was the EFF that benefited the most, arguably obstructing the DA's progress. Wards 26 (Diepkloof) and 46 (Jabulani, Soweto) in Johannesburg followed a similar trend.

In Nelson Mandela Bay, the ANC also suffered a notable erosion of its core urban black working-class vote. In Ward 56 in Motherwell, ANC support fell by about 20 per cent from 89 per cent in 2011 to 70 per cent, with the EFF taking 11 per cent from the ruling party. A similar erosion of the ANC's super-political dominance occurred in another three of my bellwether wards: 19 and 20 (Kwazakhele), and 27 (Zwide, Soweto-on-Sea).

The position in the city of Johannesburg is more complex, with apparently greater contrasts between wards. The results, like the city, are more eclectic: in some wards, for example, the EFF did especially well (winning over 30 per cent of the vote) and in other (hostel) areas the IFP achieved surprisingly good results.

It was a very big election for the opposition as well, because if they couldn't make substantial progress with the ANC so divided and badly led, when could they? It was a now-or-never election for the opposition in general, and the DA specifically. At least since the wily Helen Zille replaced the one-dimensional Tony Leon, the DA's long-term strategy has been to build step by step, town by town, city by city, province by province, proving each step of the way that it is a more reliable and capable party of government than the ANC. The major mark of progress in August 2016 was therefore not so much the share of the vote, but the acquisition of more governmental power in city hall.

The DA also had to show progress in relation to its perennial question: can it win votes from the majority community and not just from the minorities? Winning most of the rest is not a winning strategy in the long term, as the party very well knows. It has to show that it is beginning to win black votes, and at least some working-class black votes. In 2014, it doubled and even quadrupled its vote in some township voting districts, which is a bit like saying that Mali has doubled its growth rate or gross domestic product – from a very low base. We're talking about going from 2 per cent to 7 per cent in voting districts in Khayelitsha, for example. Nonetheless, the modest advances made in 2014 represented progress that the DA had to build on in August 2016.

Since 2014, the DA has acquired a black leader. Regardless of his talents, and whether he is technically up to the job, the 2016 local government elections were at least in part a referendum on whether the DA was wise to jettison the tough, uncompromising

Helen Zille for the silky but inexperienced Mmusi Maimane. This is not to say Maimane is soft. I don't think he is. On the contrary, he is capable of brave words at least. I watched, greatly impressed, when in the February 2015 State of the Nation Address debate he looked Zuma in the eye and told him, 'You are a broken man, presiding over a broken society.'[2] Culturally, it could not have been easy to look the much older man in the eye and been so brutal. In his reply a couple of days later, Zuma tried to dismiss Maimane, but did not really succeed. Maimane had made his mark and set out his own stall. (In my twenty years of watching Parliament, there have been three occasions when I have been inspired enough to immediately write a short note of congratulation and ask one of the parliamentary ushers to take it in. And this was the first time for an opposition speech; the other two were for ANC MPs.) Now Maimane had to convert his formal speech-making into something tactically adroit for the hand-to-hand fighting of a local government election campaign. He had to demonstrate that he has the savvy, and the street cred, to prove that his dulcet model-C-school accent can play strongly in working-class wards around Johannesburg, Pretoria and Port Elizabeth, while at the same time holding together an increasingly large and ideologically complex party. Neither task was, or will ever be, easy or straightforward. Maimane's lack of experience, and the sense that he has no strongly rooted ideological bearings or principles, may be exposed.

The EFF had its own not inconsiderable hill to climb. It had to show that it is substantially and not just cosmetically different from all the other start-ups that have lighted up the South African political arena since 1994, burning brightly but only briefly. First there was the UDM in 1999, then the Independent Democrats in 2004, the Congress of the People (COPE) in 2009 and, to a lesser extent, Agang in 2014. Each one has a similar story: an apparently spectacular start, fuelled by media interest; a decent but less spectacular first election result, usually 6–7 per cent (except in Agang's dismal case); followed by a dramatic and irreversible decline. They have all suffered from what sports fans will recognise as the syndrome of 'second seasonitis'. None has been able to sustain growth. Would the EFF break this mould? It is a big question, because Malema and his merry band add light as well as heat to the South African political game. One day Malema and his twenty-three red-overalled MPs will be behaving like hooligans in Parliament, disrupting proceedings in order to sustain their brand in the eyes of working men and women watching TV. The next they will be standing outside the Constitutional Court proclaiming a great victory for the country's primary liberal institution. The EFF and its leader are smarter than many expected. They have revitalised Parliament and proved to be capable of precisely the sort of bifurcated political strategy and tactics that have been lacking in the past.

And so in August 2016 the EFF had to prove that it is on the rise. Prior to the elections, I thought that anything at or around 10 per cent would be more than sufficient. Furthermore, if the EFF could position itself as kingmaker in any of the hung metros, then it would be a watershed election for the muscular third party, proving that, like it or not, Malema and his brand of populism is likely to stick around. In the event, the EFF achieved a greater proportion of the votes – just under 2 per cent more, increasing nationally from 6.35 per cent in 2014 to 8.24 per cent – but this equated to barely 100 000 more votes. The EFF did, however, and perhaps more importantly, emerge as kingmaker with the necessary leverage to negotiate its way into power in several places around the country, thereby setting up a potential springboard for future growth.

While the EFF may have impeded the DA's progress in working-class areas – a glass ceiling that the DA has to break if it is ever to offer a credible alternative to the ANC at national level – the opposition as a whole appears to have broken the mould of race-aligned voting in South Africa. This despite desperate attempts by the ANC leadership, and especially Zuma, to remind their core voters of the party's liberation credentials and history. Employing the politics of fear, Zuma used emotive language during the final days of the campaign, claiming that the DA was the child of the apartheid government and the National Party (NP). 'We cannot be ruled by an offspring of apartheid,' he said, addressing the ANC's provincial Siyanqoba rally in Port Elizabeth. 'They are snakes, the children of the National Party. A snake is poisonous and only gives birth to another snake.' Voters, however, seemed to reject these negative scare tactics, suggesting that South Africa, finally, is breaking free of the post-apartheid paradigm in which the ANC enjoyed a monopoly on political legitimacy and power.

South Africa has now entered a new era of coalition politics and government. At the time of going to print, with closely guarded negotiations ongoing at a national level, it seemed likely that in Nelson Mandela Bay, the DA would be able to form a coalition government with relative ease, with their exuberant Athol Trollip at the helm as executive mayor. There it required just four councillors from other, smaller opposition parties to side with it: those from the UDM (two), the African Christian Democratic Party (ACDP) (one) and COPE (one) provided a neat solution, given that all three parties have been yearning for coalition collaboration for years and have worked well with the DA in Parliament in recent times. The negotiations in the three Gauteng metros (Tshwane, Johannesburg and, somewhat surprisingly, Ekurhuleni, where the ANC dropped to 48.6 per cent resulting in another hung council) will have been far more complicated.

There were acute dilemmas for all the main protagonists. For the ANC, how much would it be prepared to give coalition partners in return for their support? Would it be willing, for example, to jettison its leader, Jacob Zuma – the price that the EFF was demanding as a minimum? For the EFF (and the DA), there was the dilemma of whether to even consider an offer from the ANC, given the risks associated with keeping the ruling party in power: namely, that those who voted for them because they were not the ANC might regard such a coalition as a betrayal. For the DA, could it risk an unstable coalition formation with the volatile and unpredictable Julius Malema?

In coalition politics, creativity, pragmatism, flexibility and imagination are all important factors. But ultimately the parties are answerable to the electorate, which expects clarity about the basis for any coalition agreement. The parties themselves cannot enter into coalition agreements without a clear sense of how the coalition will operate; failure to establish the rules and responsibilities of each coalition partner can quickly lead to unstable and unsustainable governance.

The country has no real experience of this sort of politics. Before 1994, of course, the NP was completely dominant. There was a rather pathetic attempt at coalition government between the ANC and the NP in the Western Cape after the 2004 election, but this was not a 'real' coalition because the NP was in its death throes and in the process of allowing itself to be gathered into the commodious political bosom of the ANC. It was more a hostile takeover of an irrelevant competitor than a partnership between two contesting political forces. As in a human relationship, a great deal depends on the relative power of the partners, and their ability either to deploy their power or to cover up their weaknesses.

Some people disagree, citing the IFP–ANC coalition government in KwaZulu-Natal in the 1990s, the DA-led coalition in the city of Cape Town after the 2006 municipal election produced a hung council and, in recent years, numerous coalitions in smaller municipalities around the country. All true. But I would argue that we have yet to enter the terrain of grand coalitions, where big beasts have to reach awkward political accommodation if they are to share power. All of the above-mentioned are fairly weak examples of coalition politics. The IFP–ANC coalition was part of a bigger, Mandela-era power-sharing arrangement that emerged from the transition-to-democracy settlement. It is true that the DA put together a complex, if unlikely, coalition of parties to give it a working majority after the 2006 municipal election in Cape Town. It was the largest single party with 90 seats, but short of the 106 it needed to have a majority. So it cobbled together an alliance with the kingmaker ACDP, which had seven seats, plus nine from other small parties (including the Freedom Front Plus, the Africa Muslim Party, the Universal Party and the UDM). It was not entirely stable and collapsed a year later, but was saved when the Independent Democrats were drawn into the coalition, ahead of a subsequent merger with the DA. While it is true that this has provided the DA with useful experience of leading a complex coalition as the

77

major player within it, it is a different proposition to be playing with bigger fish, such as the muscular, ostensibly uncompromising EFF – grand coalition politics, in other words.

What that 2006 alliance did create, I concede, was a level of political trust between the various parties, such as between the DA and the ACDP. So when the ANC leadership went into the first of many crisis meetings late on 4 August 2016 at the IEC national results operations centre in Pretoria, smaller opposition parties could be seen forming vibrant little huddles, unable to contain their excitement about becoming relevant once more, after twenty years of declining support. Indeed it was Steve Swart, an amiable senior member of the ACDP, who reminded me of how his party had built trust – a vital commodity in any stable coalition partnership – during the 2006 DA-led coalition in the Cape. Meanwhile, my favourite MP, UDM leader Bantu Holomisa, a man of invaluable sagacity and integrity in the National Assembly, looked like the proverbial cat that got the cream. He has been waiting a long time for this moment, having been the first politician to talk about a grand opposition alliance as long ago as the turn of the century.

The coalition negotiations were still ongoing as this book went to print. What will be their shape and character? Stable or unstable? Clear-sighted or blinded by a quest for the acquisition or maintenance of power? Ahead of the elections I had enormous fun asking audiences what they thought of the various permutations that would likely be on offer if either Tshwane or Johannesburg were hung: DA and EFF; EFF and ANC; ANC and DA. Which do you think is the most credible, I asked, the most realistic? Importantly – and a very different question – which do you think will produce the most effective, the best, government for the people of the city?

Regardless of the outcome of the negotiations and the basis upon which any coalition agreements are reached, it will be a good while yet before we discover whether they were wisely entered into or not. Moreover, it now looks like the country is heading towards a prolonged period of coalition politics. It is no longer unimaginable to think that in 2024, if not sooner, coalitions will have to be formed in the national sphere of government.

So let us consider the various permutations for the 2016 coalitions one by one. The DA and the EFF have been cooperating wonderfully in Parliament. The image of the opposition leaders standing outside the National Assembly after having lost their attempt to impeach President Zuma is an evocative one. Like a snowplough on the front of a train, DA leader Mmusi Maimane stands tall and proud. To his left, physically if not politically, is Julius Malema. To his right, we find the diminutive leader of the ACDP, Kenneth Meshoe. Behind him stands the UDM's leader, the father of the house, Bantu Holomisa, and Pieter Mulder of the Freedom Front Plus. Ever since the ad hoc committee on Nkandla, in which the opposition planned and executed their strategy against the ANC in close cooperation, they have offered solid yet nimble opposition. In that committee, the IFP was represented by the capable Narend Singh and COPE by Terror Lekota. It's a pity that they were not part of that photo after the impeachment debate, because it would have better captured a wider, very significant point: in recent times it is not the ANC but the opposition, altogether, who have looked like the real South Africa.

Can this be sustained into coalition government? Doubtful. Because it is one thing to actively collaborate against a common enemy – Zuma in the case of Nkandla – but entirely another to run the government of a complex city in coalition. Neither the DA nor the EFF has much experience doing so (again, notwithstanding the 2006 Cape Town council), and there is little or no institutional memory in this country on which to draw. In any case, it may be too much to ask the liberal, free-market-inclined DA to develop a workable political coalition of government with the populist EFF. It is not easy to picture them together in government, is it? Stranger things have happened, but they rarely work or end in anything other than tears.

During the year or so of their collaboration over Nkandla and related matters, the EFF has often taken the front seat, with Maimane and the DA 'tucking in behind' the fledgling party. That can't work for a city government where the biggest party – which will be the DA, in this scenario – has to show itself to be the boss. The tail cannot be seen to wag the dog. And Malema will certainly do his utmost to wag. The best, most enduring coalitions are formed on the back of a carefully negotiated programme of action based on common points of principle, with a clear sense of the non-negotiables that both unite and divide the partners. Can Maimane and Malema agree on such a thing? Do they even appreciate the need to do so? And, if not, what are the implications? It will be a rough ride for the DA, I would think, because the EFF will likely not agree to a full programme but might choose to support a DA city government on a piecemeal, one-issue-at-a-time basis. It will be pure torture for the DA. It will screw up its modus operandi of neatly proving to the electorate how much better it can govern than the ANC. Malema will take great pleasure in preventing them from doing so. It can't be in his interests to do otherwise.

So what about an EFF–ANC coalition? The ANC might be able to eat their pride – just – and do it because they will understand what it will do to the EFF brand: it will diminish Malema's unique selling point by at least 50 per cent at a stroke. His political brand is based on the fact that he is not the ANC; that he is anti-establishment and not part of the establishment, and certainly not helping to keep the establishment (ANC) in power. So unless he senses that he is going the way of the other start-ups of the past decade and that he can do better by sharing a bit of power with the ANC as a junior partner, he will resist the temptation. As the negotiations got going a few days after the 3 August elections, there was no sign that events were moving in this direction. Rather, there was evidence that Malema was fully aware of the dangers of being seduced by the ANC, setting out a list of completely unrealistic demands to the ANC leadership that included Zuma's removal and his and Cyril Ramaphosa's prosecution for the Marikana tragedy. This option, it would seem, was deliberately stillborn from the start.

This brings me to the third permutation: a DA–ANC centre alliance. As I say, strange things can happen in politics, especially in coalition politics. After all, there is very little between them ideologically or policy-wise, though both might dispute this. But coalition-building is not about ideology, a mistake that many commentators and observers made as they watched the negotiations unfold after 3 August, questioning how the EFF and the DA could possibly work together given their considerable differences in ideology and policy. Rather, coalition-building is about politics. It is about who you can trust and forge a sufficiently stable partnership with. Sometimes the chemistry of the particular leaders matters, as it did when Liberal Democrat leader Nick Clegg chose David

Cameron's Conservative Party over Gordon Brown's Labour after the UK's indecisive election result in 2010.

Going into the local government elections in August 2016, I was far from sure if the leaders of the respective parties – or the ones that will take the decisions and conduct the negotiations to determine with whom, and on what terms, their party does business – were clear about their game plan. I don't think they knew how they would handle the coalition negotiations. This was potentially very risky. To reach a deal when everyone is exhausted after a long campaign can lead to unfortunate consequences. Moreover, in countries with established traditions of coalition government – the Netherlands, Denmark and Germany spring to mind – voters also know what to expect, and parties, in general, accept a responsibility to inform the voters of what they plan to do if they are forced to enter into a coalition in order to hold power.

Thus I argued in the run up to 3 August poll that it was not only wise, but also right, that Maimane and Malema publicly explain their plans so that their voters could make an informed choice and so that their respective parties were appropriately prepared for when the moment came to sit down and talk after the votes had been counted. As the election campaign unfolded, neither was forthcoming. The DA made a clear, strategic decision not to reveal its plans – on the one hand, this was understandable, since it ran the risk of boxing them into a corner and putting off certain voters. On the other hand, the voter arguably has the right to know. After all, a swing voter who is thinking of voting for the DA may well be keenly interested in whether it would choose to keep the ANC in power or else go with the EFF and bring Julius Malema into 'town hall' government. I had an amusing opportunity to test this argument with the DA mayoral candidate for Johannesburg, Herman Mashaba, a businessman-turned-politician, when I presented as the Friday Stand-In for Redi Tlhabi on Radio 702 and Cape Talk on 20 May 2016. The interview quickly became adversarial as I challenged Mashaba, who point-blank refused to say anything about coalition plans. We turned to the callers, most of whom sided with me. The first, an ANC voter currently living in Kuwait and who planned to fly back especially to vote in Johannesburg on 3 August, said that he would now rethink his plans of switching to the DA after having heard Mashaba's refusal.

It had been over thirty years since the short-lived Lib–Lab pact of the 1970s when Britain once again faced the prospect of a hung Parliament in 2010. Although the opinion polls suggested there was a fairly high chance of such an outcome, none of the main political parties were willing to anticipate publicly what would happen. In the event, Labour got less than 50 per cent of the seats in the House of Commons and was unable to put together a coalition government with smaller parties like the Scottish National Party. Instead, the Liberal Democrats found themselves kingmakers, having to choose between Labour and the Conservatives. They negotiated hurriedly with both, but went with the Tories because they considered it undemocratic to go against the wishes of the majority who had decided against Labour.

A similar consideration applies now in Pretoria and Johannesburg. The DA and the EFF are under pressure to reach a reasonable agreement lest they disrespect the will of the majority of the electorate in those cities. Yet this will not be the only consideration. As I said, coalition-building is about the acquisition and retention of power. Displaying a charming sense of naivety, DA leader Mmusi

Maimane revealed his own incredulity about the process that was unfolding before his eyes when he tweeted on the afternoon of 10 August: 'In coalition agreements, I'm somewhat puzzled by negotiations with parties and the ANC whilst SAfricans, have voted in a #change mandate.' Welcome to the world of coalition politics, Mr Maimane – a process that will test the mettle of both sets of leaders. Make it work, and they will win the trust of the voters; mess it up, and the electorate may never forgive them and may scuttle back to the ANC quicker than you can say Nkosazana Dlamini-Zuma.

There is a serious risk that a coalition will not work and that government will break down. On the one hand, coalition government can, if the partners are mature and accommodating, produce measured, inclusive forms of responsive government that represent a wider cross-section of the electorate than when one party wins a narrow majority but behaves as if it has won with 90 per cent support. On the other hand, if there is not clarity about the rules of the (coalition) game, government can stutter along, paralysed at times, confused and contradictory at others, with the right hand appearing not to know or sometimes even care what the left is doing – much like the current national cabinet, for example, which represents at times a coalition of social democrats, nostalgic socialists, moderates, populist authoritarians, African nationalists and social conservatives (in other words, the full spectrum of the ANC, the subject to which I turn in the next chapter).

How the ANC reacts to the resounding setback of the 2016 local government elections result will be the biggest factor in setting the course for the next thirty years. This is the big question, the one for which we have been waiting twenty years to find out the answer.

The ANC was in shock and denial on the night of 4 August. The weeks and months ahead will be filled with serious introspection and repercussions, which in turn will lead to a very divisive blame game, in which Zuma and his allies will attempt to deflect responsibility. That the ANC did badly not just in Gauteng, but also in the Eastern Cape and the Western Cape (its share of the vote in the city of Cape Town, for example, fell to a dismal 24.12 per cent from 32.8 per cent in 2011), will make it more difficult for the president to do so. The ANC lost support in every province, save for Zuma's home province of KwaZulu-Natal, where the dial barely moved, from 56.57 per cent in 2011 to 57.48 per cent. Curiously in that province, the IFP gained more from the absence of the breakaway National Freedom Party (who failed to register in time for the elections) than the ANC.

Zuma may not suffer immediately and may survive a bit longer, but there is a growing acknowledgement within his own organisation that he is an electoral liability. In terms of trends, the municipal elections are a good gauge of what will happen in the national election that follows three years later. In the 2014 national election, for example, the DA got almost precisely the same share of the vote (23.5 per cent) as it did in the 2011 municipal elections, as did the ANC (62 per cent). So 2016 may be a portent of what lies ahead in 2019. The ANC leadership, especially the NEC, will be looking at this and fretting – about their own and their party's political futures – and this could shift the balance of power in the NEC away from Zuma in the coming months as the party heads towards its December 2017 national elective conference, the tricky subject to which we must now turn.

5

What next for the ANC?

When will Zuma go, and who will succeed him?

Z UMA WILL GO. It is simply a question of when. Japanese people will often tell you that they don't know exactly what is in the food they eat. The ANC is similarly mysterious. It remains as true today as when I first wrote it in *Anatomy of South Africa* in 2006: that even people inside the ANC are never sure about what exactly is happening, and why, and what will happen next.[1] Those who claim to know exactly what is happening are lying or have an agenda. The ANC is a complex, labyrinthine organisation. It is also, as my favourite senior ANC source puts it, a 'fumbling, bumbling, chaotic' one. It used to have a particular DNA, which, if you had experienced it or had learnt enough about it, could guide you in understanding what it was saying or doing, and why.

But the ANC has changed dramatically in the past ten years, and opinion is now divided in and around the organisation between those who believe it is beyond redemption and those who think it is 'saveable'. Ours is not to reason why, at least not here, in this book, because it would take up too much space and represent too great a digression from my main path, which is really to ask: what next? In the case of the ANC, this means, inevitably, asking: who's next? Leaders matter. And Zuma has mattered greatly to the ANC because, among many other failings and infelicities, he has failed to do what every other leader has achieved in the past, which is to pull together, towards the centre, the two great traditions of ANC politics – namely, its nationalist faction and its more socialist or left-leaning wing.

Thabo Mbeki held things together for a long time. But in doing so he perpetually had to dig into his political capital, which inevitably declined over time. He created too many adversaries, from the rapacious free-market, socially conservative nationalists on the far right of the ANC, to the SACP and COSATU on its left. In sustaining a broadly moderate and social democratic middle ground, he made enemies on both extreme wings of the organisation. Zuma initially brought them together under one roof, but then failed to hold them to the centre ground; they have subsequently pulled outwards rather than inwards. Was bringing them together an act of brilliance or necessity? It was necessary if Zuma was to exact his revenge over Mbeki for the latter's decision to fire him in 2005, a decision that set in motion a series of events whose final outcome is still not known. It was brilliant only to the extent that Zuma duped them. Most of them willingly joined the 'coalition of the wounded', grateful that here was a leader brave enough to take on Mbeki and with all the motivation needed to see the contest through to its bitter end at Polokwane in December 2007.

'We had to choose between a murderer and a scoundrel,' is how one ANC MP and former minister, who is one of the few who can say that he was never fully either an Mbekite or a Zumaist, put it to me. By 'murderer', he means Mbeki, whose reckless and unconscionable objection to the roll-out of HIV/AIDS treatment, and antiretroviral drugs in particular, according to some estimates, cost tens of thousands of people in South Africa to lose their lives unnecessarily. 'Scoundrel' speaks for itself. 'With Zuma, it was not so much women or drink – he's a teetotal, after all – but money. His personal finances were always in disarray,' says a former ANC exile who knew Zuma well in the years before the ANC's unbanning, when he was head of the liberation movement's intelligence wing. His relationship with money, and people with money, has always been an area of vulnerability, both for Zuma and for the ANC.

'We thought we could control him,' says another, a senior member of the SACP. For both the right and the left of the ANC, the calculation was the same: for those shunned and largely outcast by Mbeki, here was a leader who would give them the political space and the access to state power that they craved. Such has been the dominance of the ANC electorally since 1994 that to any opportunist seeking wealth, especially state resources, the ANC is the obvious route. Under Zuma, it just became easier to plunder. Almost by definition the right-wing nationalists are unconcerned by this because they are part of the rot. There is no crisis of conscience about the harm that has been done – to the ANC, to the government and to the country.

On the left, however, there is a wailing and a gnashing of teeth. There is angst and fretfulness, and, yes, at least in some quarters, a crisis of conscience. Some feel guilty that they were accomplices to this project of 'state capture' and the deepening of a culture of impunity and corruption in and around the ANC's control of governmental power. Others grit their teeth and close their eyes and construct in their mind's eye a narrative that justifies not only their original support for Zuma, but their continued presence in his cabinet. Blade Nzimande and Jeremy Cronin, respectively the general-secretary and first deputy general-secretary of the SACP, for example, have battled with this. They have faced numerous internal debates within the SACP's central committee. After the news broke in mid-March 2016 of the Guptas' influence over Zuma and the government extending to offering cabinet positions to individuals such as deputy finance minister Mcebisi Jonas, the SACP resolved that Zuma should go early. The second deputy general-secretary, Solly Mapaila, said the ANC should take action against Zuma for 'crossing the line'. 'If an ANC president can't listen to the ANC, why should he lead the ANC?' Mapaila asked ahead of the ANC NEC meeting soon after Jonas spilt the beans about the Guptas' approach to him in late 2015.

Yet Nzimande and Cronin have not resigned from government, which arguably would be the honourable and principled thing to do. It is not easy to give up power, especially when you were excluded from it for so long. They will argue to themselves that without their presence, and that of Rob Davies at trade and industry and long-time union leader Ebrahim Patel at economic development, the government will not be able to sustain its progressive policies on reindustrialisation, its Keynesian extended public-works programme of job creation and its strategic-infrastructure programme. I sympathise with their view. It is very easy to say, 'Show backbone and resign on principle!' But what further damage would that cause to progressive policy-making? Vacate the space and all you are likely to do is make it available for less progressive figures within the ANC or, worse, for yet another Zuma placeman to come in to capture the state and serve the interests of Zuma's cronies.

Why does this – the attitude of the ANC's right and left to the

Zuma years – matter? For three reasons. First, because it will impact on the succession race. Second, because it will impact on the ANC in the longer term, especially as its grip on power further weakens, as I predict it will. And, third, because it could have an impact on government policy and economic policy especially – or, at least, there is a concern or perception, particularly in the markets, that, depending on who wins the race, it could have a big negative impact.

But back to Zuma and his inevitable departure from power. I have identified fifteen possible scenarios between now and 2019 for how and when he could go, and who could succeed him and on what basis (see Figure 1). Somewhat unwisely, because it can only lead to tears – mine, if I get it badly wrong – I have attached percentage possibilities to the various scenarios. It is convoluted, because the options are numerous. I have divided my scenarios into three main 'rivers', each with many tributaries. The first – let's call it the Orange, because of its rapids and because to many it offers a beautiful and peaceful destination – is that Zuma is 'recalled' early by the ANC. This would require the ANC's NEC to decide that he should give up the presidency of the country before the end of his term in May 2019. Despite the mounting list of infelicities and political mishaps that have befallen Zuma, most of which in a 'normal' democracy would have been sufficient for him to have no choice but to resign from office, he continues to fight back forcefully. As the opposition to him – led by Pravin Gordhan and Treasury, but with significant support from Gwede Mantashe and other leaders of the ANC, including influential elders of the organisation such as Ahmed Kathrada – has increased since December 2015, so Zuma and his camp have mounted a formidable campaign of resistance in response. Both sides are strong; there is a mutually

Figure 1: ANC succession scenarios

Scenario	Tributary options	Description	Percentage likelihood	Scenario percentage likelihood
Orange	1.	Jacob Zuma ('JZ') is recalled early (between August 2016 and July 2017), and Cyril Ramaphosa ('CR') takes over	25%	
1	1.1	CR wins uncontested election at ANC national conference in December 2017		12%
2	1.2	CR wins contested election		5%
3	1.3	CR loses contested election to anon (e.g. Nkosazana Dlamini-Zuma)		8%
Zambezi	2.	JZ goes early after a special national elective conference	15%	
4	2.1	CR wins		5%
5	2.2	Gwede Mantashe wins		5%
6	2.3	Anon (e.g. Dlamini-Zuma) wins		5%
Congo	3.	JZ survives until (at least) December 2017	60%	
	3.1	JZ does not stand for third ANC presidency term	(40%)	
	3.1.1	CR elected uncontested/wins contested election	(30%)	
7	3.1.1.1	JZ recalled as president of country after CR wins		15%
8	3.1.1.2	JZ continues as president of country until 2019		15%

Scenario	Tributary options	Description	Percentage likelihood	Scenario percentage likelihood
	3.1.2	CR loses contested election to anon (e.g. Dlamini-Zuma)	(10%)	
9	3.1.2.1	JZ recalled as president of country		9%
10	3.1.2.2	JZ continues as president of country until 2019		1%
	3.2	JZ stands for third term as ANC president ('Putin Option')	(20%)	
11	3.2.1	JZ wins third term and continues as president of country until 2019, and thereafter operates a puppet president (such as Baleka Mbete)		10%
	3.2.2	JZ stands and loses	(10%)	
	3.2.2.1	JZ stands and loses to CR	(8%)	
12	3.2.2.1.1	JZ stands and loses to CR, and continues as president of country until 2019		7%
13	3.2.2.1.2	JZ stands and loses to CR, and is recalled as president		1%
	3.2.2.2	JZ stands and loses to anon (e.g. Dlamini-Zuma)	(2%)	
14	3.2.2.2.1	JZ stands and loses to anon (e.g. Dlamini-Zuma), and continues as president of the country until 2019		1%
15	3.2.2.2.2	JZ stands and loses to anon (e.g. Dlamini-Zuma), and is recalled as president		1%

detrimental stalemate, with collateral damage to the country's reputation and its global economic investment prospects.

Despite the significant setback that the ANC suffered in the August 2016 local government elections and the breaking of their political hegemony across the country, I would put the chance of an early 'recall' at 25 per cent, maybe slightly higher. Perhaps a Constitutional Court decision in late 2016 or early 2017 ordering the NPA to proceed with the corruption charges against Zuma would do it. Or some other event that one cannot yet anticipate. Although the party has been further weakened, it will take another, more drastic event to tip things over the edge. While some Zuma loyalists on the NEC will be reconsidering their position and fretting about their own political futures in the light of the local government election result, Zuma's hold on the NEC is likely to endure – just – until at least 2017.

Were he to be recalled, sometime between now and the ANC's December 2017 national conference, then, all things being equal, the deputy president – both of the country and, more importantly, of the ANC – would, like Kgalema Motlanthe in 2008, step up. Cyril Ramaphosa would become democratic South Africa's fifth president. Although this would put Ramaphosa in pole position, and with a chance to cement his leadership from the helm of government, he could face a challenge at the ANC's national conference. He could win or lose a contested election, or be unopposed. These are three of my fifteen scenarios.

The next big river – let's call it the Zambezi, because of the dangerous reptiles that may be concealed beneath the water – is even less likely (at 15 per cent): the ANC calls for a special national elective conference before December 2017. This will happen only if

(a) the NEC decides that Zuma must go, but that (b) there is insufficient consensus around Ramaphosa and/or a challenge from the right (i.e. the Zumaists). The route of a special elective conference is a dramatic one, full of uncertainty, and so predicting how things will play out is inherently precarious. Three further scenarios emerge: one in which Ramaphosa wins nonetheless; a second in which Gwede Mantashe wins because there is a divisive crisis in the party and he, as secretary-general, is pushed forward as the only man with the muscle and political reach to hold things together; or a third in which another challenger, such as Nkosazana Dlamini-Zuma, stands and wins.

The third and final river is the one in which Zuma survives, perhaps for a long time. Let us call it the Congo, because, to some people's minds, it may take us to the inevitable heart of darkness. This option now appears the most likely, at 60 per cent likelihood. In it, Zuma survives until the December 2017 national conference, and then either does not stand for a third term as ANC president and therefore gives up power to his elected successor or – worst-case scenario, but an option that cannot be discounted – tries to secure a third term as ANC president.

The Congo scenario is potentially deadly for South Africa's long-term prospects because it will likely result in Zuma remaining for his full (second) term as president of the country and only leaving at the time of the national election in mid-2019. Given how important these next three years are, the significant events that will unfold, and the economic and social pressures that are intensifying, a great deal more harm could be caused, unless the ANC leadership manages to contain Zuma very tightly in the meantime.

An even darker scenario, as a variation to this theme, has Zuma attempt the 'Putin Option', winning a third term as ANC president and then maintaining a grip on executive power in government through a 'puppet' president (as Russian president Vladimir Putin did with his 'puppet', Dmitry Medvedev, between 2008 and 2012).

Ironically, this is precisely what Mbeki had in mind when he stood for a third term as ANC president at Polokwane in 2007. Part of the Zuma coalition's case was that it was inappropriate and unhelpful to have 'two centres of power'; that once the leader's two terms as president of the country had expired, he should no longer be able to rule 'from the back seat' of the ANC presidency. Since then, the ANC has periodically toyed with the idea of turning an emerging 'convention' – that two centres of power be avoided – into a constitutional rule, but has not yet bitten that bullet, probably because there are people around Zuma with 'unfinished business' whose interests would be better served by him keeping at least one hand on the tiller of power. In fact, Zuma's decision to stay on will probably be due to a combination of pressure from these people and his own awareness that he needs to stay at the helm of the ANC in order to try to secure a compliant president in government who will protect him from, for example, the wheels of justice and/or keep alive the possibility of a presidential pardon should he ever be convicted.

The 60 per cent weighting that I give to Zuma surviving to December 2017 is split 20:40 against the chance of him trying to secure a third term and then, in the event that he does try to pull it off, a 50:50 chance of him actually doing so. I say that because Zuma will try for a third term only if he thinks both that it is necessary and that he has a reasonable prospect of winning. That, in turn, depends on how the membership chips of the ANC fall and the likely character and interests of the delegates at the national conference. In

2012 it was a done deal long before the delegates assembled in Mangaung. This time may not be much different, if Zuma continues to work the provinces that are amenable to him and his interests.

Nonetheless, overall I think this is unlikely. I don't think Zuma will stand for a third term, because he will understand that there is insufficient appetite for it in the ANC. Even some of his more venal supporters will probably take the view that he has had enough time at the top and that he should give way, not least on the basis that their interests would be better served by having an ANC president who can also take over the Union Buildings and serve those interests with the power that comes from being head of government. This takes us back to the same set of scenarios that greeted us at the end of the Orange: victory for either Ramaphosa or a challenger to him, such as Nkosazana Dlamini-Zuma.

Whether Zuma does not stand for a third term or stands and loses, there are further scenarios, which depend on whether the ANC at that point decides either to let him stay on as president of the country until the 2019 general election or to recall him outright. It might use the need to bring the terms of president of the country and president of the party into alignment as one excuse. Or else the ANC may decide that, given the need to improve its performance electorally in the light of its poor municipal election results the previous year, it would be prudent and smart to have the ANC's candidate for president in 2019 installed as president of the country for the eighteen-month period before the national election, so as to strengthen his/her hand and the party's prospects. These scenarios are fraught with complexity and potential procedural obstacles.

As can be seen from Figure 1, the 'base case' scenario – to borrow the language and concept from the world of finance and investment (i.e. the most likely outcome based on reasonable assumptions, and which falls somewhere between the best- and worst-case predictions) – is that Zuma will survive until the ANC conference in December 2017 (unless there is some extraordinary, 'black swan' event that cannot be easily foreseen at present) and Cyril Ramaphosa will win a contested election (or be elected uncontested). I put this at 30 per cent, with the prospect of Zuma continuing as state president until the 2019 election at evens (i.e. 15 per cent for each scenario).

There are other ways of looking at this intricate and confounding array of possibilities for the future of the ANC's leadership. Susan Booysen is an academic who specialises in the ANC, having written a number of books about the organisation. In a column in April 2016, she used the analogy of various famous sieges to help explain the different scenarios facing Zuma, the ANC and the country.[2]

I'd like to bring in her third, short-range siege scenario, termed 'Misrata' (after the abrupt removal of Gaddafi in Libya). This scenario, much like my Orange River one, has the ANC taking the plunge and ruthlessly removing Zuma at some point soon after the 2016 municipal elections as a result of the organisation's unprecedentedly poor result. This is not unproblematic. People say to me: the ANC was willing to act fast in the case of Mbeki in September 2008, so why not now? First of all, this fast-removal scenario assumes that there is sufficient consensus in favour of the deputy president, Cyril Ramaphosa, taking over. That consensus is conspicuous by its absence at the moment, even though since 9/12 support for him has grown among the moderate middle and social democratic left. COSATU and the SACP, for example, are now firmly behind

Ramaphosa. But that may not yet be enough. There is strong opposition from those on the nationalist right and around Zuma who want someone more 'accommodating' of their interests to replace him. The second fundamental problem is that whereas in September 2008 Mbeki had already been removed as president of the ANC (in December 2007, at the Polokwane conference), Zuma is still the ANC president, which makes him substantively and qualitatively more difficult to remove.

Procedurally, moreover, it requires the ANC's NEC to agree to remove Zuma. The NEC is largely a 'Zuma NEC', because it came in on the tide of an overwhelming victory for the Zuma slate at the Mangaung national conference in 2012. The working assumption, therefore, has to remain that Zuma does have enough support within the NEC. It is the only explanation for the NEC's decision in early June 2016 to close down the Mantashe-led 'inquiry' into the Guptas and state capture. But I see this as less of a watertight assumption than a rebuttable presumption. When I look at the list of the ANC's NEC members (see Figure 2), I do not see a list of eighty-six overwhelmingly and blindly loyal Zumaists. Going through the list and trying to identify those who are either Mbekites (of which several, such as Tito Mboweni and Thoko Didiza, were surprisingly elected onto the NEC in 2012) and/or highly principled, traditionalist members of the ANC, or those whom Zuma has alienated or otherwise upset, I count twenty-eight such names (highlighted in the list), which is almost exactly one-third of the NEC.

What triggers could tip the balance in the NEC and tilt it away from Zuma? Are there fifteen other NEC members who might find reason to shift their allegiance? The return of the corruption charges against Zuma, even if disputed and/or not followed through, will

Figure 2: ANC NEC members
(elected at the 2012 ANC national conference)

1. Zuma, Jacob
2. Ramaphosa, Cyril
3. Baleka, Mbete
4. Mantashe, Gwede
5. Duarte, Jessie
6. Mkhize, Zweli

Additional members
7. Bapela, Obed
8. Bhengu, Nozabelo Ruth
9. Brown, Lynne
10. Capa-Langa, Zoleka Rosemary
11. Cele, Bhekokwakhe Hamilton (Bheki)
12. Chabane, Collins (DECEASED)
13. Cwele, Siyabonga C.
14. Davies, Rob
15. Didiza, Thoko
16. Dlamini-Zuma, Nkosazana Clarice
17. Dlamini, Bathabile Olive
18. Dlamini, Sidumo Mbongeni
19. Dlodlo, Ayanda
20. Dlulane, Beauty N
21. Ebrahim, Ebrahim
22. Gcabashe, Lungi
23. Gigaba, Malusi
24. Godongwana, Enoch
25. Gordhan, Pravin
26. Hanekom, Derek
27. Joemat-Petterson, Tina

28. Jordan, Zweledinga Pallo (RESIGNED)
29. Kodwa, Zizi
30. Letsatsi-Duba, Dipuo
31. Mabe, Pule
32. Mabe, Sisi
33. Mabhudafhasi, Rejoice
34. Mafu, Nocawe
35. Magadzi, Dikeledi
36. Mahlobo, David
37. Majola, Fikile (Slovo)
38. Mandela, Nomzamo Winfred (Winnie)
39. Manganye, Jane
40. Maphatsoe, Kebby
41. Mapisa-Nqakula, Nosiviwe
42. Mapulane, Philly
43. Masetlha, Billy Lesedi
44. Mashamba, Joyce
45. Mashinini, Sam
46. Mboweni, Tito
47. Mfeketo, Nomaindia
48. Mmemezi, Humphrey M.Z.
49. Mokonyane, Nomvula Paula
50. Mokoto, Pinky
51. Molewa, Ednah
52. Moloi- Moropa, Joyce C.
53. Moloi, Pinky
54. Motshekga, Angie
55. Motsoaledi, Aaron
56. Mthembi-Mahanyele, Sankie Dolly

57. Mthembu, Jackson
58. Mthethwa, Nathi
59. Mtintso, Thenjiwe
60. Ndebele, Joel Sibusiso
61. Netshitenzhe, Joel
62. Nkoana-Mashabane, Maite
63. Nkwinti, Gugile
64. Ntombela, Sefora Hixsonia (Sisi)
65. Ntwanambi, Nosipho Dorothy
66. Nxesi, Thulas
67. Nzimande, Blade
68. Oliphant, Mildred N
69. Pandor, Naledi
70. Phaahla, Joe
71. Radebe, Jeff
72. Ramatlhodi, Ngoako Abel
73. Segabutla, Miriam
74. Semenya, Machwene Rosinah
75. Shabangu, Susan
76. Sisulu, Lindiwe
77. Sisulu, Max Vuyisile
78. Sizani, Stone
79. Skwatsha, Mcebisi
80. Tolashe, Sisisi
81. Tshwete, Pam
82. van der Merwe, Sue
83. Xasa, Fikile D.
84. Yengeni, Tony Sithembiso
85. Zokwana, Senzeni
86. Zulu, Lindiwe

further damage Zuma and his reputation. Some people on the NEC, no doubt, don't care and are blindly loyal to Zuma and have nowhere else to turn, but others will be concerned, and perhaps even directly affected, by the municipal elections. If they see their grip on state power, and the procurement and tender opportunities it provides, slipping, then they may reconsider their position and their future political strategy.

Who would they turn to? Who would be the 'Zumaist' candidate? It's a good question. The mainstream media has reported as if it were already a fact, written in blood and sealed in concrete, that not only will Nkosazana Dlamini-Zuma return from her stint in Addis Ababa as chair of the African Union Commission to challenge Ramaphosa, but she will also provide protective cover to her former husband and to the cronies around him who want to continue to suckle from the nipple of executive power. There are several lazy assumptions contained within this. First, Dlamini-Zuma has not yet decided to run. She is still consulting with senior figures, such as her former political mentor Thabo Mbeki. Second, thanks to the strength of the rule of law, there is absolutely no guarantee that she could provide Zuma the protection that it is said she would automatically give. And, as an acolyte of Mbeki, she is likely to be more than just mildly sympathetic to his view of Zuma and the latter's integrity, which is hardly favourable.

Third, Dlamini-Zuma is concerned that in order to run and win, as things stand, she would require the support of some of the less salubrious parts of the ANC, such as the Youth League and the so-called Premier League. The Premier League is as good a piece of evidence as any of the current plight and ill discipline, as well as the rot and rancour, that runs through the once disciplined organisation. Although they have half-heartedly attempted to deny its existence, the Premier League comprises Mpumalanga premier and ANC provincial chairman David Mabuza, who was elected as party chair for a third term in October 2015, Free State premier Ace Magashule and North West premier Supra Mahumapelo. Mabuza presides over a province in which 78 per cent of voters voted for the ANC in the 2014 national election. But it is a province that has become synonymous with political killings and allegations of corruption. Mabuza, who suffers from chronic illness, says he has 'longstanding friendships' with the other two men.[3] Given what I have been told by my sources, my sense is that at least two of these three are not people you would necessarily want to meet in a dark alley or spend time with on holiday, which is why I would prefer not to specify which two.

Dlamini-Zuma is an essentially honest person, although one of democratic South Africa's first public corruption scandals, known as 'Sarafina 2', is likely to raise its ugly head if she does stand. In August 1995 the Department of Health awarded a R14.27 million contract to Mbongeni Ngema to produce a sequel to the musical *Sarafina!* It was to be a play about HIV/AIDS ostensibly designed to resonate with the youth. The funding came from the European Union, which objected to the tender-award process and to some of the expenditure. The public protector, then Selby Baqwa, investigated and found not only that Ngema should not have got the contract and had done a poor job in delivering on it, but that Dlamini-Zuma had misled Parliament when defending the choice of service provider. As journalist Gareth van Onselen has chronicled, the case bears some striking resemblances to Nkandla, which will not add positively to Dlamini-Zuma's candidature.[4]

Is Dlamini-Zuma, in any case, up to being president? What sort of president would she be? Those who know her and have worked with her, in addition to describing her as sincere and honest, also say that she is 'managerial and technocratic', which is one of the reasons why Mbeki would have liked her. She would make a potentially decent number two; a sound deputy president. She has nationalist tendencies; she is relatively preoccupied by issues of colonialism and African nationalism. There is nothing wrong or untoward in that, but policy-wise she might not instil confidence in the markets or find it easy to be a 'one-nation' leader of the sort that South Africa so desperately needs right now during this delicate and difficult period.

Ramaphosa is a different kettle of fish. In contrast, he would be a one-nation leader. This is a man who is comfortable in his own skin and who is as relaxed in the company of a union leader as he is with a business leader, and vice versa. I remember very well the first time I heard him speak. It was soon after I had arrived in South Africa in February 1994 to work for the ANC's election campaign in the Western Cape and the country seemed to be as highly strung as a Stradivarius. Ramaphosa was speaking at the Baxter Theatre in the middle-class suburb of Rondebosch in Cape Town. The audience was middle-aged as well as middle class, and almost entirely white.

There was a buzz of nervous anticipation, which fell into a deathly hush as Ramaphosa walked in. Standing, he looked audience members in the eye, paused, released his gentle smile and said – and I will never forget the words – 'In a few weeks, we are all going to make history together.'

He paused as the audience let out a sigh of relief. People looked around; did he say 'we'? 'We are all going to make history together'? Really? Not 'them' making it for us?

It was as simple an opening line as it was brilliant. It didn't really matter what else he had to say; he had already won them over. Ramaphosa is naturally, by instinct, a one-nation leader, as evidenced by his brilliant speech to the National Assembly on 4 May 2016, on the occasion of the budget vote for the presidency, in which he called for unity in more than one tongue:

> We are living in difficult and uncertain times. It is therefore critical that we remain united in our efforts to strengthen the economy and improve the lives of our people. This is a time to instil hope, not lose hope. It is a time to shout less and share more. It is a time to innovate, not inflame. *Ye ase nako ya go lahlegelwa ke tshepo. Ke nako ya go fafatsa tshepo mo sechabeng. Ke nako ya go se hlabe lešata empa ya go fana dikgopolo tše diswa tše tse botse tse bohlale.* This is a time to do all we can to avoid the many disasters that would inevitably follow from disunity. This is a time to unite. *Nyalo sisikhatsi sokutsi sibe munye si sebentisane sibe imbumbe. Loku kutawu senta ukutsi sibe sive le somelele nale sitawu phumelela.* We should benefit from the many blessings that must flow from unity.[5]

Ramaphosa is Mandelian in that 'one-nation' sense. And his CV is extraordinary: he led the National Union of Mineworkers bravely and skilfully during South Africa's most difficult days in the 1980s; was a founder member of COSATU; was secretary-general of the ANC; and was chairman of the Constitutional Assembly, the main negotiator channel for the final constitutional settlement. And, once

Mbeki deviously, and unforgivably, pushed him away, he became a very successful captain of industry.

Of course, those last two items do not stand him well in the eyes of some; those, that is, who regard the constitutional settlement as a sell-out, or, and not necessarily the same group of people, those who regard serving on the boards of companies like Lonmin and making shiploads of money as another form of sell-out. On Marikana, he was criticised for his emails the night before the shameful massacre of striking miners, in which he asked the government to take 'concomitant action' in the face of deadly violence from some of the miners. But only someone fundamentally biased against Ramaphosa and ill-disposed to him could construe that phrase as meaning that he wanted the government's police forces to commit the murderous acts that they did.

In recent times, Ramaphosa has been doing his utmost to shore up his support. This has included carefully positioning himself to counterbalance the prevailing idea that he is 'good for business'. I have been given several accounts of meetings in which he has surprised the participants with strongly worded criticisms of business or firm defences of workers and unions. On one occasion, for example, he shocked a group of visiting businessmen from Scandinavia, who had been led to believe that he would welcome their potential investments in South Africa enthusiastically and with open arms, by giving them a lecture on worker exploitation.

People should understand that this is essential positioning as the succession race gets going. Equally, it is naive to think that Ramaphosa would be anything other than guarded in recent times. Zuma is his boss twice over: he is deputy president to him in both government and the ANC. Those expecting him to speak out publicly against Zuma, or to resign on principle, don't understand his strategy. It may appear to be overly prudential, because it is overly prudential, but to be anything else would imperil the whole point of standing on Zuma's ticket in 2012 in the first place, which was to be a moderating influence inside government and to be in pole position to succeed him.

The problem for Ramaphosa is that it is so difficult to prove a counterfactual: that things would have been even worse had he not been deputy president. And as the chairman of a major South African financial institution, who happens to be black, said to me once: another problem for Ramaphosa is that 'if you stand next to shit long enough, you end up smelling like it'.

So, if not Ramaphosa or Dlamini-Zuma, then who? ANC chair Baleka Mbete remains in the running, at least in her own mind. But her performance as speaker of the National Assembly, where she has persistently failed to cope with the EFF and has repeatedly lost control, has cost her what little support she had from the moderates and sensible left in the ANC. Like Zuma, Mbete is non-ideological; and like him, she would be a perfect candidate for those who wish to continue to take advantage of a weak, compromised president. But even if Dlamini-Zuma does not stand and Mbete is nominated by the Women's League, she would not attract wide enough support across the party to get her campaign very far.

The other options are also members of the current ANC 'top six': the secretary-general, Gwede Mantashe, and the treasurer, Zweli Mkhize. Both are, to some extent, dark horses – certainly Mkhize, who holds his cards very close to his chest. He is from KwaZulu-Natal, which is significant, and a former MEC for finance in the province. He is reasonably well liked and popular. He is quite charismatic in a rather gentle and open way. He is also ambitious. A former medical doctor, he is a free-marketeer, but could probably get support from the moderate middle of the ANC. And his role in KwaZulu-Natal gives him special power and influence within the ANC. He played an important role in sorting out the 'Nenegate' crisis in December, for example. He is an emerging kingmaker in the ANC.

Much of this analysis so far has to do with the individual personalities; the 'who' of the succession race. But what does it all mean for policy, and especially economic policy? Probably not a great deal if the more likely scenarios play out. How different would a Ramaphosa or Dlamini-Zuma administration be? Substantially, not much different. The ANC is a slow-moving creature in policy terms. Despite its fractious and fracturing features of recent times, it has remained a very stable animal from a policy perspective. Even the big ideas – like the National Health Insurance scheme – take years to percolate through the ANC system and then up and into government. If anything, the ANC is short of new ideas – or has largely run out of them – and instead continues along a well-worn path. Ramaphosa and Dlamini-Zuma might add a greater sense of purpose and direction, and focus, but they are unlikely to shift things much. The latter may put a greater emphasis on black economic empowerment (BEE), as she is more of a nationalist, but compared to Ramaphosa she may lack the aptitude, the inclination and even the skills necessary to offer convincing leadership to business and labour. Ideologically there is not a great deal to distinguish them, and at this stage neither would come into power with any great ideological '-ism' that would thrust the country onto a different policy trajectory. It would be more about governance and strategy. (Much of this can be said of Mkhize, too.)

It would, therefore, take one of the less likely, but still possible, scenarios to thrust South Africa into a drastically different policy direction. Either Zuma seizes the Putin Option with a dismal puppet state president, or Mantashe is pushed into a more muscular and populist leadership role as the ANC panics at the prospect of losing power.

Which takes us back to those river scenarios. If the Orange River flows and Zuma goes early, then Ramaphosa will take over as president of the country and put himself in a very strong position to make his case for the longer term. If Zuma is forced out as ANC president as well – another factor and complication of which to keep sight – then there would need to be an election at a special national elective conference. If Ramaphosa were to win that, then he would be in an unassailable position, at least for the foreseeable future. Were he to not win it, then the ANC – and Ramaphosa – would be in a very awkward position, effectively a repeat of the Motlanthe caretaker presidency of 2008/9, with Ramaphosa as president of the country until 2019, but knowing that the president of the ANC would take over then, in line with ANC convention.

If we are forced to paddle up and down the Zambezi or the Congo, then either the ANC will settle on Ramaphosa with Dlamini-Zuma or Mkhize as deputy, as part of a grand deal ahead of the December 2017 national elective conference, or there will be a rumbustious contest between Ramaphosa and either Dlamini-Zuma or Mkhize. A deal between Ramaphosa and Dlamini-Zuma provides the ANC with its best chance at both building unity and restoring the confidence of the country and the international community. Ramaphosa would provide the calming, one-nation leadership, with the ability to articulate a clear-minded vision to a wide number of different stakeholders and interest groups. Dlamini-Zuma could play the more 'technical' role of 'prime minister', holding line ministries to account and driving the National Development Plan in a meaningful way; such a role would suit her, and she has the strength of character and attention to managerial detail to fulfil it well. She would be the first permanent woman deputy president of the country.

As things stand, Mantashe is supportive of Ramaphosa. My view was that Mantashe would come into play as a possible successor to Zuma only if Zuma was removed as a consequence of a bad local government election result and if the EFF did especially well, causing the ANC to panic and require a more 'robust' and potentially populist leader. But Mantashe will also be under pressure *as a result* of the ANC's poor showing – for failing to secure unity and discipline in the party – and so it is unlikely that he will be an acceptable option as leader until the Zuma faction has been well and truly defeated.

Despite these complications, Mantashe remains a key figure. He runs the ANC. And however difficult that task is, he has proven in the past that he has the ability to do the necessary political fixing. He did it for Zuma in 2012, and he can do it again now against Zuma or any Zumaist who stands. The evidence suggests that Zuma's victory in 2012 was the result of a weak challenge from Kgalema Motlanthe, one that never really got off the ground due to Motlanthe's lack of ruthlessness and hunger for the top job, but more so because Mantashe was able to cook the books so effectively.

The ANC's electoral college is comprised mainly of delegates who are nominated by branches, proportional to their volume of members, with extra votes cast by representatives on behalf of the ANC Youth League and Women's League. Mantashe announced in the run-up to Mangaung that KwaZulu-Natal – Zuma's stronghold – had gained some 87 000 new members since the beginning of 2012, up from 244 900 members to 331 820, out of the ANC's total membership of 1.2 million. Meanwhile, the Eastern Cape – the potential fertile ground for a (non-Zulu) challenger to Zuma – had been going in the other direction: at the beginning of 2012, it was hot on KwaZulu-Natal's heels with 225 597 members, but by September, when the final tallies were done by the ANC leadership, the Eastern Cape had mysteriously slid to just 187 585 members.

This meant that about 38 000 members had left the party in that province, or had not paid the R12 required to renew the annual membership. Mantashe attributed the Eastern Cape's decline to serious organisational problems, which is plausible. However, the decline of a province hostile to Zuma's re-election has raised eyebrows. Limpopo also grew, from 114 385 to 161 868 members, as did North West, from 60 319 to 75 145 – both provinces that were largely supportive of the incumbent, but no less dysfunctional than the Eastern Cape – if anything, more so. The North West was probably the ANC's most dysfunctional province. It had two distinct camps that were at war. Before that, the province was run by a task team led by people from other provinces and deployed by the ANC's NEC. With all that confusion, they still managed to attract 15 000 new members.

The membership trends would have been a big deal if the NEC had accepted the suggestion that branches be allocated voting seats at Mangaung as a proportion of their membership size. That would have seen KwaZulu-Natal being allowed to send more than 1 000 delegates. But that format was rejected at an NEC meeting, where it was decided that each branch must have at least one delegate, as per the ANC's constitution. So, in terms of the 4 500 delegates that were supposed to vote at Mangaung, Eastern Cape went down from 877 in 2007 to 676 in 2012; KwaZulu-Natal, however, went up from 606 to 974. Zuma had won even before the buses bringing delegates to Mangaung had arrived.

Hence, those wishing to see where the balance of power in the ANC lies now will need to watch these internal ANC processes, and especially the numbers game, with great care. The detail matters a lot. The KwaZulu-Natal ANC is now greatly divided, certainly more so than before, and Mkhize is critical to this. Indeed, in late May 2016, a very significant shift in the balance of ANC power in KwaZulu-Natal played out when the premier, Senzo Mchunu, was 'recalled' by the party. Intra-party politics are especially murky in KwaZulu-Natal, and highly dangerous: there have been numerous political assassinations in the past year. But the decision suggests a big victory for the nationalists/Zumaists and a defeat for the moderate middle/sensible left, since Mchunu was aligned with COSATU and the SACP in the province.

In terms of the proverbial elephant in the room that is ethnic politics, there is a lot of conjecture. But certainly the fact that Ramaphosa is not Zulu may be to his advantage. There is concern within the wider party about Zulu dominance, just as there was concern from KwaZulu-Natal about the 'Xhosa-nostra' dominance of Mbeki's time, overstated though it in fact was. Mkhize will have to take this into account when deciding where to place his support.

If he supports Dlamini-Zuma on an all-Zulu ticket, it may weaken both their chances. Support Ramaphosa and it could be a winning ticket, provided that they can keep Mantashe fully behind them. Ramaphosa, in turn, might promise Mkhize that he will be president for only one term and appoint Mkhize as minister of finance. This option, similar to the Ramaphosa–Dlamini-Zuma one, offers the ANC the possibility of escaping both the nightmare and decline of the Zuma years, and the pain of a deeply divisive succession battle.

But the other known unknown is whether Zuma will be brought down by the criminal justice system. Although deeply contaminated by his determination to control the prosecutorial authorities, now that the High Court has ruled that the decision to drop the charges against Zuma in 2009 was irrational and unlawful, the NPA is faced with a delicate decision: whether or not to prosecute a sitting president. Do they have the guts to do so? Or will this Teflon president once again dodge the bullet? As we will now see, whoever succeeds Zuma may end up having to make a very tough call.

6

A delicate time, in a dangerous year ...

Where to from here for Number One?

ADDRESSING THE CONSTITUTIONAL COURT in the Nkandla case, Advocate Jeremy Gauntlett memorably said it was, for his client, 'a delicate time, in a dangerous year'. Whether Gauntlett was referring simply to the Nkandla matter or was speaking of the wider political context with municipal elections on the horizon, only he knows. But it neatly captured the current state of Zuma's world. For soon enough, Zuma may find himself in need of a Gauntlett, or someone just as able, to represent him in criminal proceedings. In late April 2016, the North Gauteng High Court handed down judgment in a case with potentially even greater political consequences than the Nkandla Constitutional Court judgment – namely, the judicial review application brought by the DA against the decision taken in April 2009, shortly before the election that brought him to power, to drop corruption charges against Zuma.

The court ordered that the decision to drop the charges was taken without a rational basis and, therefore, unlawfully. It has put considerable further pressure on the president, as well as on the National Director of Public Prosecutions (NDPP), Shaun Abrahams, who one way or another will have to decide whether to proceed with the prosecution of Zuma. This will fiercely test Abrahams's independence; the perceived wisdom is that he is Zuma's lackey, having been appointed by the president in 2015.

Again, a brief reprise of the history is necessary and appropriate. This matter stretches back to the last century. However, I vividly recall as if it were yesterday the sight of then NDPP Bulelani Ngcuka striding around like a peacock at the ANC national conference in Stellenbosch in 2002. He was accompanied by Leonard McCarthy and Willie Hofmeyr, who at the time headed up key parts of the Scorpions – the so-called untouchables, the investigating unit into serious and organised crime that was established by the Mbeki administration, but which was dismantled by Zuma after he came to power because he perceived it to have been part of the witch-hunt that was conducted against him by Mbeki and his henchmen, Ngcuka and McCarthy. At Stellenbosch, the three gentlemen were wearing dark glasses, dark suits and dark ties. But for Hofmeyr's scrawny build, they could have walked off the set of *Men in Black*. Rather indiscreetly, they were discussing their investigation and how it had led them to Zuma and how they were going to take care of him. It related to Zuma's relatively modest involvement in the infamous arms deal, whereby South Africa had procured in the late 1990s around R70 billion worth of weapons, fighter planes and warships that it arguably did not need in return for various bribes that were made to individuals and to the ANC itself.

But when the moment to prosecute Zuma came, the National Prosecuting Authority blinked. In 2003, Ngcuka announced that although there was a prima facie case against Zuma, they would proceed only against his 'business associate', Schabir Shaik. The charge sheet had been set up for a joint charge against both men, but at the last minute, for reasons that are still unclear, Zuma's name was literally tippexed out. A year later, after the 2004 election, Mbeki re-appointed Zuma his deputy president. A year after that, in June 2005, Shaik was tried and convicted and given a long prison sentence. Zuma slipped away – legally, at least – to fight another day.

But then Mbeki decided to bring Zuma's political career to a drastic halt, and fired him on 14 June 2005. Given that he so often tolerated or turned a blind eye to the scandals or infelicities of members of his cabinet and other leading figures in the ANC, the question of why Mbeki decided to act so decisively against Zuma is not an easy one to answer. On the face of it, the judgment against Shaik, delivered by Judge Hilary Squires, provided sufficient grounds. Although Squires never actually used the well-known phrase that the press subsequently attached to the matter – namely, that Zuma and Shaik were in a 'generally corrupt relationship' – there was plenty of evidence that Zuma had behaved inappropriately.[1]

But Zuma had not actually been convicted of anything; he was guilty by association. And the matter was inevitably going to be appealed, as indeed it was (though doing so did not help Shaik, who was later sentenced to fifteen years in prison). And so Mbeki must have had a political motive for removing Zuma. The reasonable supposition is that he did not trust Zuma and did not want Zuma to succeed him, which, because he had been elected deputy president of the ANC at its national conference in Mafikeng in December 1997, he would have done.

Regardless of Mbeki's precise motive or thinking, it was a momentous decision that set South Africa's politics onto a completely different trajectory. If Mbeki's aim was to remove his deputy from the political future, and kill off his chances of becoming ANC president and then president of South Africa, then he failed completely. Paradoxically, Mbeki sowed the seeds for his own destruction at Zuma's hands. At an all-time low, Zuma shuffled off to lick his wounds. He then carefully but swiftly built a strong, anti-Mbeki coalition that included COSATU and the SACP, exacting revenge by defeating his cerebral opponent at the ANC's national conference at Polokwane in December 2007. The ANC would never be the same again.

Mbeki fought back; he may have lost the presidency of the ANC, but he was still president of the country. On 28 December 2007, just days after Polokwane, Zuma was re-charged, but these charges were mysteriously dropped in early April 2009. In the interim, Mbeki had fallen on his sword after the ANC's NEC decided that he should be 'recalled' in September 2008, and he resigned as president of the republic. Again, the catalyst for such a dramatic and drastic political event was a court decision. This time it was the Eastern Cape High Court and Justice Chris Nicholson who perhaps unwittingly made their mark on political history and shifted its course. Nicholson went out of his way – unnecessarily and inappropriately, the Supreme Court of Appeal later said – to describe the political conspiracy that had been directed against Zuma. This, in essence, rendered the prosecution fatally contaminated and, therefore, unlawful. On 12 September 2008, Judge Nicholson granted Zuma's application to have the corruption charges against him dismissed. Released from the threat of criminal prosecution, at least for the time being, Zuma memorably told his supporters that, as far as Mbeki was concerned, 'when the snake is dead there is no need to cut it in half'. As many of us have now come to understand, often when Zuma says something like this he means or intends the opposite. His supporters proceeded to cut the snake in half: just eight days later, Mbeki was turfed out of power.

If Mbeki's decision to fire Zuma in 2005 had vast implications for Zuma's future, Nicholson's had an even greater and certainly more immediate consequence for Mbeki. When Nicholson's judgment went on appeal shortly thereafter, the SCA attacked the judge with rare ferocity, finding that on the issue of political interference he had gone off on a frolic of his own and that the court had 'overstepped the limits of its authority'. On this basis at least, the decision to recall Mbeki was unjustified. On the substantive issue, the SCA found that Nicholson's interpretation of section 179 of the Constitution was wrong and that the NPA was under no duty to invite representations from Zuma before re-charging him. Accordingly, the charges were reinstated from the date of the SCA's judgment on 12 January 2009. But this was to prove a short-lived victory for justice.

At the press conference announcing the decision to discontinue the prosecution of Zuma just three months later, the nervous acting NDPP, Mokotedi Mpshe, spoke in general terms about the prosecution process having been tainted by 'political interference' from former Scorpions boss Leonard McCarthy, but was vague and far from convincing about the legal basis for the decision to discontinue. Sitting alongside Mpshe was Willie Hofmeyr, who had somehow escaped his association with Ngcuka and McCarthy sufficiently to ingratiate himself with the new regime and had risen to be the deputy NDPP. Though he has been pushed to the margins of the NPA and is no longer deputy NDPP, Hofmeyr somehow survives to this day. As someone who knows him well once said to me, Hofmeyr 'runs with the foxes and hunts with the hounds'.

That now infamous NPA press conference took place on 6 April. The DA acted fast, filing papers in the North Gauteng High Court the next day, 7 April 2009. The case, dubbed 'the spy tapes case' by mainstream media, was finally heard in early March 2016. That it took seven years to get to the hearing was due primarily to Zuma's legal team's skill in filibustering. Ironically, given the reckless things that Zuma and his loyalists in government and the ANC have said about the judiciary, he benefits greatly from the strength of the rule of law in South Africa and from his adept use of legal procedure. If this was Russia, or any other of several emerging markets, Zuma would have been imprisoned long ago.

The spy tapes case hinges on whether a decision to discontinue a prosecution is judicially reviewable and, if so, whether the decision to drop charges was made on a rational, and therefore lawful, basis. The DA argued that the decision to discontinue the Zuma prosecution fell within the definitional ambit of 'administrative action' contained in section 33 of the Constitution and section 1 of the Promotion of Administrative Justice Act 3 of 2000 (PAJA), and as such is reviewable by the High Court either in terms of the Constitution or in terms of section 8(1)(c) of PAJA. In 2012, the SCA decided that it did not need to decide this question since Zuma and the NPA had conceded that any exercise of public power, including a decision to discontinue a prosecution, was liable to a 'rule of law' review – that is to say, that it conforms with principles of constitutionality and public accountability.[2]

In politics, eventually your chickens will come home to roost. The North Gauteng High Court is not well disposed towards Zuma and his administration. After all, this was the court that the government lied to over the al-Bashir matter. Courts don't like being lied to, especially by a democratically elected government. Unfortunately, while the court was decisive in its reasoning about the main issue – the rationality and lawfulness of the decision to discontinue the prosecution of Zuma – it was not terribly clear about the impact of its finding. Immediately after the judgment was delivered on 29 April 2016 by the deputy judge president, Aubrey Ledwaba (a fine example of the new generation of admirable young judicial leaders in South Africa), there was argument and confusion as different interpretations of the judgment were debated in social media and elsewhere. Our view at CASAC was that 'the only logical and sound interpretation of the High Court's ruling is that it restores the situation as it was immediately before the decision to discontinue the charges was taken: namely, that as things stand, President Zuma is indicted with numerous serious charges of fraud, corruption and racketeering'.[3]

On this interpretation, NDPP Abrahams has no decision to take. The charges are reinstated. All things being equal, the NPA should proceed with the prosecution of Zuma. CASAC stated: 'If we are to be in a situation where the NDPP must consider whether to reinstate the charges, then there was no need for the Court's order. The NDPP could have been approached directly to consider reinstating the charges.'

Not everyone agreed, however. The ANC put out a statement saying that as far it was concerned, because the decision to discontinue the prosecution had been put before a court, it would require a court decision to restore the charges. But this is nonsense. In its judgment, the court stated at paragraph 93: 'The respondents further argued that since the charges against Mr Zuma were formally withdrawn in court on 8 April 2009 after Mr Mpshe decided to discontinue the prosecution the order sought in the notice of motion [by the applicants, the DA] may be of no consequence. We are constrained to state that said technical argument was not raised in the papers and it cannot render the order we are to make herein inept and ineffective.'[4] In other words, there is no merit in the argument that it would take a further court order to reinstate the charges. The court put it succinctly: 'Mr Zuma should face the charges as outlined in the indictment.' And, as CASAC's executive secretary, Lawson Naidoo, put it in the organisation's media statement: 'The grievous consequence facing South Africa now is that we have a sitting president, recently found to have violated his constitutional obligations by the constitutional court, now also facing 793 counts of corruption and related offences. The nation must now contend with the political and constitutional implications that flow from this.'

On 23 May 2016, Abrahams announced his decision to appeal the High Court ruling. However, courts do not always grant leave to appeal. The test is whether there is a 'reasonable prospect of success'. On 24 June, the High Court therefore rightly refused to grant leave to appeal. Now the NPA must try its luck with the SCA. Since the core issue – whether a court can judicially review a decision not to proceed with a prosecution – has already been ventilated in the SCA in the Mdluli matter,[5] which was a trial run for the Zuma case, it is difficult to fathom that the court will see any merit whatsoever in an appeal on the same point of law. The NPA will then be forced to go directly to the Constitutional Court, which will likely grant leave on the basis not only that it does not have the authority to overturn the SCA precedent, but also that the matter is of such great public interest that it requires the highest court in the land to rule.

This would then put the matter off until late 2016 or early 2017. Zuma, via the NPA, can kick the can down the road for a while, but sooner rather than later the matter is likely to come back to the NDPP, who will *have* to make a decision about whether or not to proceed with the prosecution. Hopefully, the Constitutional Court will have clarified the position and ruled that the charges are 'live' once again, and that the prosecution should proceed unless the NDPP finds new grounds upon which to discontinue (he can't use the same ones as before, as those have already been held to be 'irrational').

The delay notwithstanding, the case will put Zuma's integrity once again in the spotlight. It will persistently remind everyone that he was due to face very serious corruption charges. And again, it will put the ANC leadership in a difficult position: should it continue with such an obviously flawed and dodgy leader or risk the turbulence that will come from jettisoning him early?

The problem for Zuma will be this: even if he can sustain the narrative that the Mbeki regime was out to get him and that this tainted the NPA's approach at the time to prosecuting him, it does not necessarily impact on the merits of the case. If there is evidence against Zuma, with a reasonable prospect of success, the prosecution should succeed. Zuma should get what he has always claimed he wants: his day in court.

The ANC leadership will not be the only ones under pressure. NDPP Shaun Abrahams will face the toughest decision of all. He is the first lawfully appointed NDPP of the Zuma years. Deliberately, or at least recklessly or negligently, Zuma has attempted to appoint a series of entirely inappropriate people as NDPP. Not since the second NDPP, Advocate Vusi Pikoli, was suspended by Thabo Mbeki in 2007 (because the president was upset that Pikoli proceeded with the arrest of veteran ANC strugglisto and police commissioner Jackie Selebi) has the NPA had a permanent, fit and proper NDPP. Mpshe acted until 2009, when Zuma appointed Menzi Simelane notwithstanding the serious findings that the Ginwala Commission of Inquiry (into the suspension of Pikoli) had made against his veracity. The DA challenged the rationality of the Simelane appointment and won. Thereafter, for eighteen months the divisive and toxic Nomgcobo Jiba acted. It was only when CASAC threatened legal action to force President Zuma to make a permanent appointment, to end the instability that was undermining the operational integrity of the prosecuting authorities, that he appointed Mxolisi Nxasana to the position of NDPP in October 2013. This did not go well either. Nxasana also had a shady past, in that he had failed to disclose his prosecution for murder, for which he was acquitted, and his conviction on two assault charges. He was duly suspended as NDPP and then paid off. So it was only in mid-2015, after eight years without a fit and proper permanent NDPP, that Abrahams was appointed.

Will he be up to the task of deciding whether to prosecute a sitting president? Abrahams has a track record of conducting tough prosecutions, as the first NPA 'insider' to be appointed as NDPP, but he will be put under enormous pressure by the pro-Zuma camp to avoid making the decision. The appeal of the High Court decision may 'stay' the matter and give Abrahams some breathing room, at least for a year or so, by which time the whole game may have changed. If not, the question of presidential immunity may also raise its head. The assumption is that, because the Constitution does not say that an incumbent president is immune from prosecution, he is not. However, when one looks around the world – and the court may take foreign law into account – common practice and jurisprudence is that when the law is silent, it is taken to mean that there is presidential immunity. In one scenario, Zuma's legal team runs this argument, initially as a further delaying tactic that would necessarily have to go all the way up to the Constitutional Court. And they may even succeed.

Such an outcome will just shift the decision-making to another era. Whoever succeeds Zuma will find himself or herself head of a government that will have to decide whether to proceed with the prosecution of Zuma. While in theory the government may not interfere with the prosecutorial independence of the NPA, in practice there may be pressure to drop the charges again or else even to go as far as offering Zuma a presidential pardon, which, in turn, would probably be subjected to judicial review. And so it will go on. Even if he lives to a hundred, Zuma may well find that he continues to spend an inordinate amount of his remaining days on this planet in the company of his lawyers.

There are a number of big decisions that lie ahead and which will impact on the next three years and beyond. First, the Constitutional Court will likely have to decide whether it agrees that the April 2009 decision to drop the charges against Zuma was irrational. Second, it must decide whether to order reinstatement or 'merely' that the NDPP reconsider doing so, in which case, third, NDPP Abrahams will have to decide whether to reinstitute those charges. Fourth, the ANC will have to decide whether the return of the corruption charges is a tipping point that tilts the political equation finally against Zuma and that they can no longer sustain having him as president. Fifth, there is the question of whether or not Zuma does enjoy presidential immunity. And finally, if he does, there is the matter of how his successor handles the question of his prosecution and the possibility of granting a presidential pardon.

The uncertainty about Zuma's corruption case serves to further diminish his already lousy reputation, both at home and abroad. Number One is not taken seriously by the market, by at least half of his party, by most public servants and, now apparently, by the majority of the population of South Africa. Only those who fear Zuma continue to respect him. And his ability to instil fear and loyalty with seductive and irresistible inducements should not be underestimated. That trademark giggle, the feigned bonhomie, and the populist song-and-dance routine should fool no one. He is a ruthless and dangerous manipulator, of people and of truth. This only adds to South Africa's political uncertainty at a time when it can least afford it. It is a delicate time in a difficult year and there are risks everywhere you look.

7

Risk on, risk off

Team Treasury and the
pivotal role of Pravin Gordhan

K NOW WHAT A 'risk off' is? No? Well, don't worry; nor did
I until a couple of months ago. I had provided a group of
investment bankers and emerging-market analysts with a picture
of South Africa's political scene and likely scenarios looking ahead,
when, for the last few minutes of the dinner, they turned inwards,
towards their own obscure, complex world. A question was posed.
It sounded like it included the word 'riscoff'. Presumably not a
cheap instant coffee, but what was it? A place in Russia, a person,
some kind of market mechanism? I may not have understood the
question, but the answer was clear enough: it was a straight tie
between Turkey and South Africa.

The reason seemed to be that in both cases the 'macro' was vul-
nerable. In South Africa, the structural constraints were too severe
and the current account made things especially delicate. 'Macro'
includes political risk, as well as a country's broad economic policy
and international trade story. The 'current account' is the broadest
measure of trade in goods and services. In the last quarter of 2015,
South Africa's current-account deficit increased to 5.1 per cent of
gross domestic product, up on the forecast of 4.4 per cent. Why?

Because exports – so important to the South African economy, especially in commodities – had fallen despite a rapidly weakening rand. Bloomberg reported in March 2016 that a 'worsening in the trade outlook threatens to undermine the rand further after it fell 11 percent against the dollar in the past six months. South Africa relies mainly on foreign investment in stocks and bonds to help fund the current-account shortfall, inflows that declined in the fourth quarter as investor confidence in President Jacob Zuma's administration weakened.'[1]

Which takes us back to politics and its relationship with economics and market sentiment and conditions, and, thereby, the dinner-table conversation. A 'risk off', I learnt, was a term of art, developed by market analysts and traders in the aftermath of the 2008 global financial crisis, when traditional low-risk, reasonably high-yield developed markets no longer offered the same degree of certainty. Investors were more inclined to take greater risks in searching for yield, and emerging-market economies were the inevitable beneficiaries, notwithstanding any macro risks attached to them. As a result, a new lexicon emerged: 'risk on, risk off'. This captured the herd-like tendency of the market to move collectively towards higher-risk markets and then, suddenly, to run away from them. So, the question that was put to the assembled traders at my dinner was this: if there is a 'risk-off' retreat from emerging markets, which country's currency would you sell first?

In spite of the comparative competitive advantages, such as the quality and strength of its rule of law, the depth of the country's capital markets and the quality of its corporate leadership, South Africa's economic structural constraints carry more weight. These include what the market regards as too high a cost of labour, relative to its skills; relatedly, the quality of the education system, or lack thereof; the costs of doing business – for example, the red-tape bureaucracy that faces small businesses or the labour-law safeguards that protect employee rights and make it unjustifiably difficult, in the eyes of some employers, to dismiss inadequate workers; and the inefficiencies and inadequacies in infrastructure that supports key industries, such as mining, and which therefore constrains exports, negatively impacting on the balance of payments and the apparently critical factor, the current account.

The internal contradictions of these factors always intrigue me. Typically, investment bankers or market analysts will first ask me about Zuma (What's going to happen? Who will succeed him and when? And what will it mean for policy?); then, something about the opposition (they would prefer to see more competition and less chance of a 'slide' to a one-party state); third, a question about the unions and the price of labour (they would prefer wages to remain low); and fourth, they ask about social stability and inequality (they would prefer stable conditions in which to do business, notwithstanding the also-stated need to keep wages low). This is not a circle that can be squared. But I have come to realise that it is not the function of such people either to be reasonable or to provide solutions to the inevitable contradictions. Theirs is a simple, hardnosed calculation: where, and on what relative basis, will I get a better return for my client's money?

This analytical approach inevitably puts a country like South Africa in a very awkward position, to say the least. The year 2016 is especially awkward because of the confluence of political and economic risk. The fact is that while the economic conditions – globally and locally – are hardly congenial, the politics, and especially the conduct of President Zuma, makes things far worse. The Zuma administration invariably shows mixed signals on its attitude to the market in general and to private-sector enterprise specifically. This is partly because there are free-market liberals in the cabinet – some of them also hard-line nationalists – alongside social democrats who want to defend the welfare state that the ANC government has built since 1994, and (former) socialists who not only believe in a strong state, which they now couch in terms of the Asian Tiger concept of 'the developmental state', but are also fundamentally and instinctively ill-disposed towards private profit (namely, trade and industry minister Rob Davies and Ebrahim Patel, minister for economic development).

But there is ambivalence within the ambivalence. Davies and Patel often speak the 'right' language of private–public partnership and the need to increase private-sector participation in their industrial revitalisation and infrastructure-building projects – the two pillars that stand as the policy justification for the left's broad support for Zuma back in 2007 – but when it comes to implementation, things often do not move as fast as they should because there is not actually a wholehearted commitment to using public subsidy to catalyse private-sector investment, unless it comes in the form of smaller, less ideologically inconvenient packages. But 9/12 was a wake-up call. There was a sudden realisation that you can't sustain a big social-security safety blanket and a big public-investment infrastructure strategy alongside big industrial subsidies if your public finances are in disarray. Seeing Davies – possibly the most left-wing member of the cabinet – begin his defence of the State of the Nation Address in the debate following Zuma's speech in mid-February 2015 with an ardent and apparently heartfelt eulogy in praise of 'fiscal discipline' was quite remarkable evidence of this shift.

While Pravin Gordhan's leftist critics would say that this is because he has been 'captured' by the 'neoliberal' Treasury and their friends in the international finance sector, Gordhan, however, really does get it. Writing on his return from the 2016 spring meetings of the World Bank and International Monetary Fund (IMF) in Washington DC, Gordhan wrote a strong, clear-minded piece in the *Sunday Times* asserting his belief that 'without the private sector investment growth is a challenge' and arguing that despite the constraints on monetary-policy accommodation and expansionary fiscal policy, where South Africa can do little or nothing at the moment, there were still important structural reforms that the country could undertake.[2]

But before scrutinising those structural reforms and their importance for the future, allow me to pause for a moment and dwell on Gordhan's Budget Speech on 24 February 2016, because it was a speech we had needed to hear for several years. It was presidential; it was, in so many ways, the real State of the Nation Address, as opposed to the typically feeble and dull-minded one delivered by President Zuma a couple of weeks before. What Gordhan did that Wednesday afternoon was draw a line in the sand. Which brings me to a revealing semiotic moment, this time of the purely linguistic variety. Halfway through a speech that showed extraordinary political leadership and courage, Gordhan, despite his previous denials, used the 'P word' – not 'privatisation', but 'predator'. For the uninitiated, the word might seem at best curious; at worst, obscure and confusing. To the connoisseur, it is what one might call a 'trigger' word, drawn as it is from the leftist literature on revolutionary class struggle. In that literature – some of which was ventilated, ironically, by SACP leaders such as Blade Nzimande and Jeremy Cronin, two of the ministerial beneficiaries of Zuma's political largesse in the years after Polokwane – the notion is raised of a comprador class that eats away at the revolutionary integrity of a political movement and adopts predatory conduct in respect of the use of state power (think tenderpreneurs and public procurement).

So, by use of that word, Gordhan was speaking truth to power: *we know what is going on and now, finally, we are saying, 'No more'.* It represented a defiant throwing down of the gauntlet and a potential turning point. It was, therefore, an uplifting moment. Indeed, sitting in the press gallery, I had feelings of pride and optimism for the first time in a long while. I felt like applauding, but I restrained myself because commentators must not only be impartial, they must be seen to be so. Yet, inwardly I don't mind confessing that I was excited and proud. Excited that someone was finally standing up and showing the kind of political leadership the country needs. Proud of South Africa's ability to provide such leadership and proud of the ANC and its own capacity for leadership.

As such, it would be apt to assess Gordhan not just for his performance as minister of finance, but also as the figurehead or vanguard of a revival of what I like to call the moderate middle and sensible left of the ANC, because it is clear that he has considerable political backing from those parts of the party and that that backing is of great political significance both for the immediate future and in the longer term.

But what, exactly, are they backing, apart from Gordhan himself?

What are the 'structural reforms' that the minister of finance is pushing through? In this context, it is worth remarking on Gordhan's own use of the phrase 'structural reform'. It is ideologically loaded, reverberating as it does with the 'neoliberal' 'Washington-consensus' approach to government that was the hallmark of the 1990s and which has attracted so much angry criticism from the left. Some of those critics regard Gordhan as a neoliberal. Patrick Bond, for example, penned a long lament after the Budget Speech that complained bitterly about the cuts that Gordhan had introduced, but said not a word about what he should have done instead and how, in fact, Gordhan was supposed to maintain South Africa's welfare state without finding a way to balance the books.

Ironically, the market reaction to the speech was underwhelming. Clearly some investors and market analysts wanted or expected a more front-loaded and deeper fiscal plan, with more austerity and higher taxes. But that was entirely unrealistic. Gordhan did make cuts (R25 billion over the next three years), in that he essentially told his colleagues that not only was he freezing the replacement of senior staff, in order to cut the public-sector wage bill, but he also could not guarantee that their line items would not be cut in the future. At the same time he explicitly confirmed that three areas of public expenditure would be ring-fenced from cuts: namely, education, as the single most important investment for the future (with an extra R16 billion allocated to higher education over the next three years, funded through reprioritisation of expenditure plans); infrastructure, as the current single best way for the government to influence economic growth and protect jobs (R870 billion is committed for the public infrastructure programme over the next three years); and the emergency response to the drought. The way

Gordhan justified these three areas was clear-minded and clearly expressed, and therefore impressive and persuasive.

More importantly, Gordhan built on his core platform of fiscal consolidation, to tackle corruption head-on. On the former, he said this: 'We cannot spend money we do not have. We cannot borrow beyond our ability to repay. Until we can ignite growth and generate more revenue, we have to be tough on ourselves.'[3] Interwoven in the speech was a set of structural reforms that can be summarised as follows:

- Cutting wastage in the public sector and reducing the public-sector wage bill, against the backdrop of the very expensive public-sector wage deal that was reached in 2015.

- Fiscal consolidation: a determination to continue to balance the books and not spend what government does not have (including on nuclear power).

- Governance of state-owned enterprises (SOEs): a stated recognition that, as Gordhan put it, the 'strength of our major state-owned companies does not lie in protecting their dominant monopoly positions, but in their capacity to partner with business investors, industry, mining companies, property and logistics developers, both domestically and across global supply chains'. In addition, the governance of several SOEs, including the controversial board of South African Airways (SAA), will need to be urgently reformed.

- Create space for new private-sector participation in the economy: 'It seems clear, furthermore, that we do not need to be invested in four airline businesses,' said Gordhan. This was not 'privatisation', because, clearly, this would not be a good moment to sell state assets, given both the state of those assets and the state of the market, but rather to begin to fatten the turkey for Christmas by introducing minority equity partners.

- Cut red tape for small businesses – the budget introduced a number of institutional mechanisms for doing so, against the backdrop of a stated commitment to listening to businesses' real concerns – and introduce some labour reforms.

At whom was this directed? His colleagues in government? Partly. The public and other social stakeholders? Yes, to an extent. The rating agencies? Very much so. Gordhan went on a whirlwind road-show of developed-country markets a fortnight after the speech, to London, New York and Boston. In the *Sunday Times* a week later, three of the representatives of business who accompanied Gordhan – Christo Wiese, Cas Coovadia and Colin Coleman – penned a piece in which they, too, set out a laundry list of items that they optimistically argued needed to be accomplished in the following three months – i.e. by mid-June, the time of the rating agencies' mid-year review and the first of two key moments when South Africa might face a downgrade to 'junk status'.[4]

The list reads as follows (and is worth setting out as an exposition of the sorts of things that the private sector and the investment world are looking for, and what the rating agencies will be looking to for signs of progress):

- fix legislative impediments to investment, including 'resolving the "once empowered, always empowered" legislation' relating to BEE ownership of at least 26 per cent of mining company shares introduced in 2002 by the mining charter;
- agree on some key labour reforms with social partners, including an appropriate minimum wage;

- re-equitise Eskom to strengthen its balance sheet;
- execute the proposed merger of SAA and SA Express and the introduction of a minority shareholder into the government's airline businesses;
- announce the principle of a minimum of 40 to 50 per cent of all SOE boards to come from the private sector, as a way of remedying their weak governance;
- act on establishing the small- and medium-sized enterprise venture-capital entrepreneurship fund as a partnership of business and government, funded by both;
- consolidate the social compact between the government, labour and business that 'was so positively received by investors during the roadshow'; and
- work with businesses to announce new capital projects across industry.

This set a tough assignment, especially given both the tight timeline and the political economy that has to be navigated in the case of many of the reforms – i.e. the vested interests, whether of the government, the private sector, cronies around Zuma, or labour unions who hold dearly to the labour laws of the mid-1990s that represented such an important victory to them and which they are loath to dilute. Part of Gordhan's job will be to construct a narrative of progress that reflects the toughness of what he is trying to do and helps those who are evaluating his performance to do so fairly.

They say you should never waste a crisis. And in one important respect, Gordhan, exploiting the opportunity presented by the 9/12 crisis and his appointment, has forged a new relationship between business and government. On that front, his reform project is making very good progress, having established three government-business-labour working groups that are focused on (a) doing the right things to avoid a rating-agency downgrade; (b) creating a R4 billion fund for small and medium enterprises to help them grow and provide employment opportunities; and (c) conducting a sector-by-sector analysis of the economy to explore the growth opportunities and identify constraints. Obviously the third objective is more long term, but a leading member of one of the working groups (a CEO of one of the big four banks) told me that he was very positive about progress with (a) and (b), and that almost half the R4 billion had been raised, on the basis of a fifty/fifty split with government. Moreover, in his view, relations between government and business were 'better and more productive than they have been for fifteen years'.

Unfortunately, regarding the first item on Wiese, Coovadia and Coleman's list – fixing legislative impediments to investment – things have not gone so well. The mining sector, already under great pressure due to low international commodity prices and demand, has been fretting about the 'once empowered, always empowered' principle. It was the Mbeki administration that in 2002 unilaterally, and with very little prior consultation, announced a BEE framework for mining companies, wherein 52 per cent of all shares were to be black-owned. It was the equivalent of pushing a fox into the Nkandla chicken coop. The hens ran around headless for a short period before the realisation dawned that this was, in fact, merely an opening offer. A couple of months later, the government settled on half that: 26 per cent. Since then, the mining sector – still an important prism through which South Africa's economy is viewed by international investors and emerging-market analysts – has operated on the assumption that this figure of 26 per cent was a once-off deal; that 'once empowered, always empowered'.

The matter is now before the High Court, the Chamber of Mines having submitted an application for a declaratory order around these very ownership clauses in the Mining Charter (though moderates within the ruling party, such as head of the ANC's economic transformation committee Enoch Godongwana, have been pressing for and, in Godongwana's case, actively seeking to broker a settlement). Yet, notwithstanding this and the new *entente cordiale* between the private and public sectors that was the backdrop to both the State of the Nation Address and the Budget Speech in February, the minister of mineral resources, Mosebenzi Zwane, took it upon himself to upset the apple cart. On Friday 15 April 2016, Zwane decided that the eve of the spring meetings of the IMF and the World Bank was the perfect moment to table a unilateral amendment to the Mining Charter that would unequivocally vanquish the 'once empowered, always empowered' principle. At the time, Gordhan was in Washington to promote his fiscal consolidation and structural-reform initiatives. In the prevailing climate, it was hard not to smell a rat. Was it a deliberate attempt by some of his cabinet colleagues, or their backers, to undermine Gordhan yet again? Let us not forget that the Hawks dispatched their twenty-seven questions relating to the South African Revenue Service (SARS) 'rogue unit' days before the February 24th Budget Speech, a story worth reviewing here.

First, I must point out a recurring problem with the Zuma administration: the incoherence of its cabinet. Because of a lack of decisive leadership at the top, or even a kitchen cabinet with the requisite skills and capacity to fill the void around the president, cabinet ministers are invariably free to pursue their own agendas. Often the left hand does not know what the right is doing, sending confused signals to business and potential investors. Rent-seekers have a largely open field, too. And Zwane is associated with those rent-seekers, having been appointed in circumstances similar to those of Des van Rooyen, in that Zwane's predecessor, Ngoako Ramatlhodi, was summarily dismissed in September 2015 without any good reason. As *Business Day* reported: 'A number of senior mining figures, speaking on condition of anonymity, said Mr Ramatlhodi's departure could not have come at a worse time and criticised the fact that Mr Zwane, who appears to have little or no experience of the sector, was linked to the Gupta family. "It was one thing Ramatlhodi being pushed to another ministry by the president, but it's another having someone with baggage or a perception of baggage at this critical time for the industry," said a senior executive.'[5]

Unlike the Van Rooyen appointment a couple of months later, neither the ANC leadership nor business nor anyone else was able to step in and stop Zuma from acting so recklessly in appointing such a crassly obvious placeman as Zwane. It should have set off the biggest alarm bells. It speaks volumes that it did not. And it is hugely revealing both of the state of the ANC and its loss of control – at least at that time – over its president and of the fact that he had 'gone rogue'. Although 9/12 presented a low point from which the only way was up, and indeed a new, positive political trajectory was embarked upon, it was always clear that it would not be a linear journey; there would be a twist and a turn in the story to follow.

The first came immediately before the Budget Speech in which Gordhan so emphatically laid down the law, when current SARS commissioner Tom Moyane – Zuma's man at the government tax revenue agency that had begun to close in on the president and his family and friends with its investigations – began to wage war against Gordhan through the proxy of a bogus 'investigation' by the police fraud unit, the Hawks. Successor to the Scorpions, the Hawks is itself led by a dubious Zuma appointee, Lieutenant General Berning Ntlemeza, whose posting has been challenged by the Helen Suzman Foundation on the grounds that he was unlawfully appointed because he is not a 'fit and proper person'.

In the short term, it will be essential to see whether Gordhan is able to withstand the various attempts to intimidate him. By early June, Gordhan appeared to have seen off the Hawks by answering their twenty-seven questions, thereby calling their bluff. The questions relate to a decision to set up a specialist intelligence unit within SARS around a decade ago. The reason – which most people will fully understand and support – was to give the agency the teeth and muscle to be able to investigate effectively, especially the most serious serial tax dodgers. Gordhan, then SARS commissioner, appointed a former comrade from the struggle days whom he trusted to lead the unit – deputy commissioner of SARS Ivan Pillay. No one can really second-guess this decision. Indeed, then minister of finance Trevor Manuel signed off on the funds needed to run the unit. However, things went a little rotten when the unit allegedly hired some old-school intelligence operatives from the apartheid era who may, it is not hard to imagine, have gone about their business in, well, the style of old-school intelligence operatives from the apartheid era – that is to say, with little acquaintance with, or consideration for, the law. Allegedly, they tapped phones without permission and generally proceeded in a rogue fashion –

thus earning the unit the sobriquet 'rogue unit'. The question is whether Gordhan knew enough about these operational details to be held responsible and accountable for them now. It seems unlikely. It is more likely a smokescreen for an attempt by the Zumaists to undermine and intimate Gordhan. But Gordhan will prevail. Indicators of whether I am right will be that the Hawks back off; Tom Moyane is 'redeployed' within months or even weeks; and the SAA chairwoman, Dudu Myeni, who is believed to be 'close' to President Zuma – and certainly heads his rural foundation – is removed.

Myeni was one of the reasons that Nene was summarily removed on 9/12. Against the wishes of National Treasury, who had taken on responsibility for the government's shareholding in SAA (a move that had a senior Treasury official wryly observing to me in early 2015 that 'we now seem to be in the airline business'), Myeni sought to restructure a deal with Airbus over the lease or purchase of new aircraft. But the main reason was nuclear power.

The thickest line in the sand that Gordhan has drawn is over Zuma's apparent obsession with procuring nuclear power and to do so from Russian state-owned enterprise Rosatom. Gordhan has stated very clearly that the government will not procure what it cannot afford. Zuma spent a lot of time with Russian president Vladimir Putin in the first part of 2014. Every time I bumped into a certain National Planning Commission (NPC) commissioner in an airport or at a conference, he would whisper in my ear: find out how many times Zuma has met with Putin this year. Apparently more than a dozen. Zuma personally took charge of the nuclear decision-making process on the back of the 2010 resolution – now overtaken by events, such as lower demand for electricity because of the slump in the economy and greatly reduced costs of renewable energy – to include 9 600 megawatts of nuclear power in South Africa's future energy mix. The decision to proceed with this was confirmed by cabinet in 2015 and, curiously, in a government gazette dated 24 December, the procurement process was formally commenced, notwithstanding the fact that Treasury has not yet completed an affordability study. Merry Christmas!

The concern is not just that circumstantial evidence suggests that a massive bribe will be paid by the Russians to Zuma, and perhaps to the ANC, but that South Africa will enter into a power-purchase agreement on the back of a vendor-financed capital-expenditure agreement, and that the commitment to buy electricity from the (Russian) company for perhaps twenty or thirty years will lock South Africa into a price that its economy simply cannot afford. Sources in the Department of Energy informed me last year that they had been told to 'get the deal done, as quickly as possible, and don't worry about the procurement rules; the presidency will provide cover'. Thus, the nuclear-procurement issue will be a huge fault line, not just for Gordhan and his credibility, but also for South Africa's democracy and public accountability. It is one to watch very carefully over the next year.

These are smaller, though still enormously important, sub-questions of a bigger one, not just for 2016, but for the next three years and beyond: can Pravin push through his reform package? The reason why the answer – positive or negative – will reverberate far longer is that, as the nuclear-deal question illustrates so well, there are huge economic and political implications either way. In the shorter term, there are other questions to consider. What if Gordhan is unable to provide the rating agencies with convincing evidence that sufficient progress is being made on his reform package? A downgrade will inevitably follow. What will the implications be? And to return to where I began: What if there is a risk off? Will South Africa follow Brazil into a dizzyingly disastrous downward spiral? Can the centre hold? And, perhaps the biggest question of all: Can Gordhan make it to 2019? Because we need him to outlive Zuma politically; that much is clear.

8

Will the centre hold?

Reasons to be cheerful … and gravely concerned

S OUTH AFRICA GOT itself into a rut. The slide was incremental, not sudden. It happened over a number of years, from around 2005 onwards, as government began to get tired and run out of ideas, and as it became apparent that the deeply rooted structural constraints of the economy presented intractable obstacles to real progress. When the commodities boom cycle turned towards bust, and the global economic crisis blew its chill wind southwards after 2008, things became even more difficult. Increasingly, I found myself struggling to maintain a positive outlook as investors and market analysts asked me the same question: South Africa's stuck, isn't it, and there's no real sign of it breaking free from its constraints, is there?

I was forced to agree: South Africa was in a rut. There were few new ideas. From the ANC government there was more of the same, despite the best intentions of people like Rob Davies and Ebrahim Patel with their reindustrialisation and public infrastructure strategies, and Trevor Manuel and his NPC's admirable yet sadly unrequited National Development Plan. But the same was not enough. And, worse, the hard choices were not being faced let alone taken: labour market reform to make it easier to employ young people; standing up to the arrogance of the teachers' unions in the face of their defence of the indefensible – bad teachers; arresting those responsible for stealing state resources; and halting state capture.

And then the Zuma years worsened as a crisis in political leadership emerged along with a bleak truth: the ANC had made a disastrous choice in 2007 and ended up with a man who is not only unfit to head a modern government, because he cannot be bothered to read the bare minimum of documents needed to lead and chair a cabinet properly, but is also deviously corrupt.

Did we notice and, if so, did we act? Those are the questions for everyone with the responsibility that comes with power and privilege. Did we do enough to stop the rot? And as I asked myself, and others, these questions, another truth, with an apt metaphor, dawned: with its scandal fatigue, South Africa was like the proverbial frog gently boiling in the pot. South Africa could not get out of its rut partly because it did not realise it was in one. It could not confront its worst failures because it was not fully aware of the damage that was being done. Slowly, inexorably, the country was boiling alive.

And then along came 9/12. Relief can sometimes come in strange packages. Zuma's reckless, dangerous and damaging decision to fire Nhlanhla Nene set in motion a series of events that could yet bring redemption and set South Africa on a different course. I say 'could', because there is a cold war playing out between Zuma and his cronies on the one side, and the reform group led by Pravin Gordhan on the other. Battles are being won and lost, by both sides, almost on a daily if not weekly basis. It is not yet clear who will win the war, but the outcome is crucial. Depending on the victor, South Africa is faced with two very different narratives.

So, to turn to the last of the six questions that this book identi-fies as critical not just for the short term, but for the long term as well: will the centre hold?

This was one of Thabo Mbeki's favourite questions, drawn from a poem by his most treasured poet, William Butler Yeats. Mbeki was fond of deploying it, along with other poetic utterances, in his speeches. It was, however, never clear to me whether Mbeki was asking the question of his party or his country, or perhaps both. Do we not miss him now, with his apparent erudition and sincerity of purpose? As the Zuma years unfolded, in the wry words of one friend of mine, 'we discovered that we are all Mbekites now'.

Maybe not everyone. The ANC left has to live with the conse-quences of their decision to support Zuma and help bring him to power. But it also brought them into the cabinet in far greater numbers than under Mbeki, and, as one of them – Ebrahim Patel – drily observed to me as he filed out from the 2011 State of the Nation Address: 'I don't miss the poetry.'

Having made their bed, they have decided to continue to lie in it. Everything is relative, and in politics, as in life, you must always be careful what you wish for. And so, just as many were glad to see the back of Mbeki, now, as a result, we are saddled with a leader who is a wanton vandal. But Mbeki's recent attempts from early 2016 onwards to rewrite history with a typically bizarre sequence of Facebook missives about his time in office remind us that he was very far from perfect, too. Nevertheless, his rhetorical question – will the centre hold? – and the stanza of the poem from which it is drawn – 'The Second Coming' – provide a rather neat framing for a consideration of the question of what next for South Africa as a society:

Things fall apart; the centre cannot hold;
Mere anarchy is loosed upon the world,
The blood-dimmed tide is loosed, and everywhere
The ceremony of innocence is drowned;
The best lack all conviction, while the worst
Are full of passionate intensity.

This book has to some extent been about the first part of the first line: *Things fall apart*. The caveat is that its thesis is not that things have definitively fallen apart, but rather that they are falling apart and that there is an intense contestation going on that will determine whether the decline can be arrested or not.

There are reasons for being cheerful; I remain fundamentally optimistic. Why? What, in the face of so much foolishness and squander, when so many people fear that South Africa has begun its descent towards a dark place that some liken to Zimbabwe, can justify optimism?

First, there is the strength and quality of some key institutions, such as the public protector, the National Treasury and the South African Reserve Bank, as well as the higher courts. The courts, and especially the Constitutional Court, have stood up to the test. The chief justice is prepared to lead; as the outgoing deputy chief justice, Dikgang Moseneke, said on his retirement: '[Mogoeng's] are safe hands'.

Second, South Africa has a strong and resilient civil society. The notion of civil society means different things to different people. Often 'civil' society can be thoroughly 'uncivil'. What it means to me is the social forces that operate in and around, and outside, the main institutional and organisational sectors of government and the private sector; in other words, anything that is outside the state and which is not concerned with making a profit. In this, South Africa is richly endowed thanks to the churches, the non-governmental movement of NGOs and law centres, community structures and the trade unions (though, sadly, COSATU is far weaker than it was five years ago).

This overlaps with the third factor: South Africa's people, its 'human capital'. It is so often said that South Africa's labour market is underskilled and overpriced. That may or may not be entirely true. And, certainly, the failure of decades of public education policy to prepare ordinary citizens for a competitive labour market is a disaster. But South Africa's professional classes are highly skilled and resilient. They are a thick layer of quality fat at the top end of society, not a thin layer of cream as is the case in many other developing or emerging economies. They find expression in different ways: in the depth of the legal profession, for example, and in the IT or banking sectors, and also in the quality of corporate leadership. South Africa's equity market is stable because investors see strength in the way South African businesses are led and managed.

Fourth, there is cause for hope in that the moderate middle and the sensible left are finally finding their voices and summoning the courage and resolve to stand up to Zuma and the craven nationalists and authoritarian populists within the ruling party who are venally intent on destroying so much of what has been achieved since 1994. There is reason to believe that both inside and outside the ANC there are people and structures – including Julius Malema and the EFF – who can constrain the worst tendencies within the ANC and around Zuma.

Fifth and finally, a new generation is emerging, again both inside and outside the ANC, that is not trapped by the past and that can look critically at what is happening and take action. I see this vigour in my students and in the student protest movement. Of course, there is unwelcome violence at times, and immaturity and crudeness in the logic of the arguments advanced, but that is to be expected of the young (at the risk of sounding both old and patronising). But the fresh thinking and energy is entirely welcome and needed, and encouraging.

We shall soon see whether all this optimism is justified.

But there are also plenty of causes for grave concern.

For things to *really* fall apart, what does that involve and mean? What will it look like if it gets to the point that *the centre cannot hold*? First things first. Above all else, it will mean that the crisis in political leadership not only continues unabated, but further contaminates the economic governance sphere. That process has begun, and continues to creep in and around the institutions of economic and financial management, but is being pushed back.

The Zuma-versus-Gordhan tussle lies at the heart of this. It is, for once, not an oversimplification to present it in such terms. Gordhan is trying not only to defend the integrity of the public finance system and the organisational strength of National Treasury, but also to push back the venality of 'state capture' that is represented by the Guptas but which is not – alas – limited to them. Battles over the control of state-owned enterprises such as SAA and Denel continue.

A great deal will depend on who wins. If Gordhan loses, then the implications are too great and too many to enumerate. But it is a necessary exercise to try to undertake, so let me attempt it.

The first point is to recognise that the rating agencies are watching carefully. They have a shopping list of items where they expect to see progress. They, and to some extent the market in general, are willing to give Gordhan the benefit of the doubt, at least for a while. But patience will quickly run thin, and remorselessly; the not-so-invisible hand of global economic reality will squeeze South Africa.

This will not be pretty, economically or politically. Regardless of what one thinks about the madness of the way in which the global financial system is organised, one has to acknowledge certain realities. Economically, the consequences of a downgrade to so-called junk status would potentially be very serious. Government borrowing, already relatively high, would become more expensive, as South Africa would be required to pay a higher interest rate in global markets. This would put further pressure on the national fiscus as more public money would be spent on servicing government debt.

Inflation, already on the increase because of 'imported' inflation due to the run on the rand in the latter part of 2015 (which was significantly worsened by Zuma's decision to fire Minister Nene, a prime example of bad political leadership impacting on the economy) and the rise in food prices due to the drought, would further increase, hurting the poor the most as basic foodstuffs and other essentials become more expensive. Interest rates would likely rise, as the South African Reserve Bank seeks both to protect the currency and to constrain inflation, putting downward pressure on the economy as borrowing money and domestic bonds become more expensive, further decreasing consumer purchasing power and reducing demand, thereby slowing down growth and confidence.

In short, a vicious economic cycle would follow. Some of these factors will likely kick in regardless of whether a downgrade occurs in December 2016. Inflation, for example, rose to 7 per cent in February (though it had dropped to 6.1 per cent by June). When people who are already under great pressure find that they can no longer afford basic foodstuffs, they will inevitably get angry as well as desperate. Protests will follow. And they are likely to be furious and violent. They could interfere with domestic politics, as the various issues become intertwined and as a local political economy involving the corrupt use of state resources at a local level, such as tender processes, is threatened.

Thus: *Mere anarchy is loosed upon the world.*

What are the ingredients of this potential, Brazil-style descent, where negative political and economic components collude to create a perfect storm? There are seven main factors. The first is political leadership. Leadership – and the lack of it – always matters. As this book has sought to point out, the political leadership of South Africa has failed the country. The Zuma years have turned into a nightmare, far worse than anyone could have reasonably expected.

If only it were just one man. Part of the destruction that has occurred with the acquiescent disregard, or active encouragement, of Zuma himself has been the dismantling of institutions, primarily through the choice of leadership for those institutions: the National Prosecuting Authority, the South African Revenue Service, South African Airways, the Hawks, the Department of Mineral Resources ... the list goes on.

As we have seen, a line was finally drawn when this acidic contamination of important institutions reached National Treasury on 9 December 2015. But by then a great deal of harm had already been done.

The second key factor is the state of the economy, both global and domestic. As trade and industry minister Rob Davies is fond of saying, 'Men make history, but not of their own free will.' In other words, context is everything. And, granted, the economic context of the last few years has not been congenial. Now we have come to appreciate Trevor Manuel's prudence even more. The far left constantly criticised the former finance minister, who held the position for a record thirteen years from 1996 to 2009, for his unwillingness to spend all of the funds available to the government. He preferred to save for a rainy day. Well, that day has come. And things would be far worse if he had been more spendthrift and had also failed to instil in National Treasury a resilient culture of fiscal rectitude.

Notwithstanding this, the global financial crisis of 2008/9, combined with the sharp downturn in commodity prices, on which South Africa and so many African and other developing-country economies are still too dependent, resulted in increases in unemployment and severe constraints on growth. Those conditions largely persist, so further buffeting from the drought, for instance, or fluctuations in the exchange rate have an even greater adverse effect than they would ordinarily.

Thirdly, therefore, the country has faced very tough choices in terms of the core macroeconomic relationship between public expenditure, public borrowing and revenue. As I observed in the previous chapter, those choices are getting tougher. There is very little room for manoeuvre. There are going to be cuts in public expenditure. If economic conditions worsen, and government's budget further contracts, then eventually it is likely that welfare spending may have to be cut, threatening the already impoverished existence of millions of South Africans and increasing the likelihood of violent social protest.

Fourthly, as the analysis of Karl von Holdt, one of the best social researchers in South Africa, has shown, local community protests have spread across South Africa since 2004, with a dramatic upsurge in 2009 and 2010 as the negative impact of the 2008 economic crisis kicked in. 'At the same time,' he writes, 'protests have become increasingly violent, marked by the destruction of public and private property, and confrontations between armed police and stone-throwing crowds.'[1]

His report, entitled 'The Smoke that Calls' – such an evocative and compelling title to a piece of seminal research – concludes 'that rapid processes of class formation – through which, on the one hand, a new elite is emerging and, on the other, a large underclass of unemployed and precariously employed, together with the dislocations of the transition from apartheid to democracy – is generating fierce struggles over inclusion and exclusion both within the elite, between elites and subalterns, and within the subaltern classes themselves'.

By mid-2016, the student protest movement appeared to be in 'sleep mode', as if someone had pressed the pause button. But just as many of us were taken aback by the intensity and resilience of the student-led protests in 2015, so we should not be surprised when the movement rises up again. Universities are likely to remain on the front line. As so many times in the past, around the world and in the course of human history, it will be the student movement that acts as a powerful vanguard for the struggles of the day.

Von Holdt reminds us also that the struggle against apartheid during the 1980s established violent practices as an integral element of civil society mobilisation and of struggles for citizenship, so 'it is not surprising that similar repertoires of violence are apparent in current insurgencies over citizenship and exclusion'. Inevitably, therefore, violence will be turned against non-South African members of such communities; outbreaks of xenophobic violence are, sadly, likely to be a regular feature of the social landscape in the coming years, further undermining South Africa's reputation, especially on the continent.

A fifth factor is the specific contextual character of local government and local politics. A dangerous political economy has entrenched itself over the past twenty years, in which, as ANC stalwart Yunus Carrim described it to me for *The Zuma Years*, there is a congealing embrace between ANC office holders in branches, ANC control of local government and ANC people who run businesses whose dominant business model is the winning of local government tenders. As Carrim put it back in 2012: 'In a sense local government is a concentrated expression of the country's problems as a whole. While there are some problems with the local government model, and changes are going to be made, the core principles, values and features of the model are, I think, sound. But until we have a more stable, strong and cohesive ANC it's going to be difficult to sort local government out.'

Since 2012, despite the efforts of the national government to try to get a grip on local governance and financial performance, power struggles within the ruling party have undermined these attempts. 'Power struggles within the party,' Carrim said back then, 'are translated to municipalities and serve to undermine good governance and service delivery in municipalities. But, also, power struggles within municipalities get transferred to party structures and serve to weaken the party.' This chimes with 'The Smoke that Calls', in which the case studies indicate that 'the ANC itself, as the locus of many of these struggles and contestations, has become a profoundly unstable organisation. This has ramifications across state and society. These very dislocations, instabilities and contestations in social relations, and in the meanings of these relations, tend to give rise to the practices of violence in struggles over social order and hierarchy.'

Moreover, the sixth factor, this instability within the ANC has become increasingly violent. As a fellow member of CASAC's executive committee, Ebrahim Fakir, drily observed in response to an invitation to discuss possible violence between parties in the local government election campaign, 'that assumes that the ANC stops fighting amongst itself'. Fakir made his throwaway comment in May 2016. In June, things got a whole lot worse, as the ANC's factional infighting descended to unprecedented levels of violence in Tshwane. I say 'unprecedented' because this is the first time that widespread violent protests, causing retail groups such as Massmart to close stores, have originated directly from disputes about the ANC's choice of candidates for the local government elections. When the party announced its mayors for the metros in mid-June, there was dismay in some provinces. In Tshwane, ahead of the announcement, incumbent mayor Kgosientso Ramokgopa was not on the list of three candidates given to the ANC provincial executive committee. His deputy and the leader of the rival faction, Mapiti Matsena, was – representing a grouping hopeful of getting 'its turn' in power. In an attempt to forge unity in the region, Luthuli House then parachuted former Mbeki cabinet minister Thoko Didiza in as mayoral candidate. It backfired spectacularly, adding to the sense that the ANC has lost control.

Research by Professor Mark Shaw, a prolific and accomplished expert in the field of criminology, shows the shocking extent to which assassinations have become a part of the socio-economic and political landscape in South Africa.[2] His research reveals over a thousand cases of organised 'hits' since 2000, which were 'aimed at removing particular individuals, and sending wider signals about power relations to promote a variety of political, economic or criminal interests, or all three combined'. Adds Shaw: 'They are also deeply symptomatic of the broader challenges of corruption and rent seeking in South Africa.'

Writing in *Business Day*, Gareth van Onselen noted in 2013 that '[a]nyway you cut it, on average, at least one politician has been assassinated every month in South Africa for the last five years'.[3] He pointed to the reporting of Genevieve Quintal, who estimated that as many as forty-six people across all political structures were assassinated between 2007 and 2012. As Van Onselen pointed out: 'The *Daily Maverick* estimates there have been 59 [political killings] in the last five years. And an internal ANC report claims 38 of its members have been killed in KwaZulu-Natal alone since the beginning of 2011 – excluding 13 Inkatha Freedom Party and National Freedom Party members killed during the same period.'

Seventh, and lastly, there is the violence of the state itself. Under Zuma, the role of the intelligence services, and of state security generally, has become more pervasive and more violent, as well as more clumsy. I have seen it for myself in Parliament: first, as state intelligence services took over the organisation of accreditation for the State of the Nation Address, which led to the farcical moment when the cellphone signal was blocked by state intelligence an hour before the start of the address in February 2015 as part of its crude attempt to lock down the National Assembly in the face of anticipated disruption from the EFF. Second, when the EFF persisted with its interference in President Zuma's attempts to deliver his speech, it was not Parliament's own security officials but a specially prepared and trained group of police officers who entered the chamber to violently remove the EFF MPs. I saw them for myself earlier in the day turning up for their final briefing. They were cops. And they should not have been permitted to enter the chamber. Both of these incidents raised serious questions about separation of powers and Parliament's own independence. But Zuma's 'authoritarian populism', to use the very apt phrase of political scientist Professor Vishwas Satgar, does not care about such democratic niceties. And his police force does not care about policing in a peaceful manner befitting a free and democratic society. The number of deaths at the hands of the police has increased markedly since 2009. Marikana was the murderous pinnacle of this authoritarian trend.

As social protest increases, so will state violence in response. A Zuma administration, unwilling or unable to build social consensus or a new social contract, will resort to its own authoritarian, heavy-handed crackdown. In this, the ANC under Zuma has lost sight of its political register. Now, it is one-dimensional in its political response, trapped by its own ineptitude and unable to escape the cycle of rent-seeking state capture, institutional decline and authoritarian response to civil society's complaints about corruption and the failure to efficiently deliver public services.

And so, in this dark scenario, *the blood-dimmed tide is loosed*. As South Africa seeks to find space to celebrate the twenty-year mark of its constitution, so cynicism and disappointment will dominate: *Everywhere the ceremony of innocence is drowned.*

But South Africa has had plenty of experience of teetering towards the brink, taking a good, long look over the edge, and then pulling itself back to fight another day. Which takes us, finally, back to the last part of Yeats's stanza: *The best lack all conviction, while the worst are full of passionate intensity.* Part of the (relatively) cheerful thesis of this book is that 'the best' have begun to find their voice and to fight back, having for so long lacked the conviction necessary to resist the intense venality of those who have ruthlessly exploited the political leadership vacuum of the Zuma years.

Corporate South Africa must do its bit. They must have their say and exert their influence, but constructively and with an appropriate note of patriotic duty as well as outrage. The rich must do their bit. They must give more, in terms of time as well as money. Moreover, however unappetising, South Africans should not turn their backs on politics. They must engage and get involved. The choice is simple: be a bystander and, thereby, an accomplice to the downward spiral or, rather, be a protagonist, a contestant, one of those who rolled up their sleeves and stood in the path of history. That is the choice for individual South Africans and for the country.

CONCLUSION

Six questions and six answers

As well as two scenarios for the future
and nine signposts along the road

W HAT WILL HAPPEN next? How exactly will the next three years unfold so as to set the course for the next thirty? It seems clear that South Africa has reached a fork in the road. The year 2016 has been a big one: we've witnessed an authoritarian populist Jacob Zuma cling to power in order to continue to loot the state, and wage war against a reformist finance minister, Pravin Gordhan, who in response has attempted to draw a line in the sand and say 'No more' while at the same time trying to convince sceptical rating agencies that South Africa should not be downgraded to junk status. We've observed the political traffic warden, ANC secretary-general Gwede Mantashe, biding his time, knowing that Zuma has become far too politically expensive, and yet unsure as to how, or when, to plunge his knife into the back of his president to complete the much-needed coup d'état by the moderate middle and sensible social democratic left that until recently has succumbed so meekly to Zuma's state capture. We've been faced with an unforgiving market and unyielding global and domestic economies. And we have been left with an increasingly angry population, and a vanguardist, militant student movement, ready to pounce and to lead a South African Spring in which the centre will decidedly not hold. The ruling party has lost its way and abandoned so many of its great traditions and principles, and, without a united trade union movement as an ally, it is unable to absorb the socio-economic pressures that unbendingly press against South Africa's stability, increasing political risk and turning investors away. The opposition tread unsteadily forward, hoping to benefit from the ANC's travails and division, yet unsure of the policy agenda and political strategy that will differentiate them sufficiently from the establishment, other than to claim that they will govern more efficiently and more honestly, as if that alone will fix South Africa's deep structural economic constraints.

And yet, as I say, there are reasons to be cheerful. It is make-or-break time. There is a 'make scenario' and a 'break scenario', and not a great deal in between. But first, to return to the guiding conceptual framework of this book: at the beginning I posed six questions that I averred would be decisive in setting the course not just for the immediate future, but for the next three decades or more. Now, in conclusion, I must try to answer them.

First, will the key institutions, especially the judiciary, hold the line? Yes, they will, though some crucial appointments that are to be made in the next year will be critical: two Constitutional Court judges, and Public Protector Thuli Madonsela's successor.

Second, having made serious inroads into ANC hegemony in a game-changing set of local government elections in August 2016, can the opposition kick on and make the most of their progress, and what will be the likely implications for the opposition, for the ANC and for a new era of coalition politics? Thanks largely to

Zuma's divisive and corrosive leadership, now that the ANC has fallen from its perch, it will prove very hard to put Humpty Dumpty back together again. Unless the opposition make a complete mess of coalition government – which is entirely possible – there is every reason to the think that they can kick on and that South Africa's competitive multiparty democracy will further consolidate. Whether, however, this produces better government and better prospects for South Africans, especially the poorest citizens, is another question.

Third, how will the ANC respond to the election outcomes and who will succeed Zuma? I honestly don't know. It depends on whether Zuma can be contained or, better, removed from power at the first available opportunity. In turn, that depends on whether the ANC's moderate middle and sensible left can turn its new resolve into action. It really is, finally, a battle for the soul of the ANC, and much depends on the balance of power within the ANC's national executive committee. While I want to believe that the organisation can reboot and recover its good, old traditions, I fear that it is too far gone and that, regardless of who succeeds Zuma, the ANC is unlikely to play the nation-building, progressive role that it once did and provide the country with the unifying leadership that is urgently needed if South Africa is to contend effectively with the multiple socio-economic constraints that undermine prosperity, stability and social justice. Progress will come in spite of the ANC, not because of it.

Fourth, will the Constitutional Court effectively box National Director of Public Prosecutions Shaun Abrahams into a corner, forcing him to pursue the prosecution of President Zuma and thus precipitating Zuma's early departure from office? I doubt this will happen, not because the courts won't play their part, but because a combination of Zuma's legal filibustering and political manipulation will prevent the wheels of justice from turning sufficiently fast. Even if he is prosecuted and then convicted – a lot of ifs, with many a slip between cup and lip – his successor will then face a tough choice if there is pressure for him or her to pardon Zuma. But by then he finally will be out of office and, thankfully and hopefully, with the Zuma years over, South Africa can recover some of its dignity, reputation, and sense of principle and purpose.

Fifth, perhaps the biggest and most important question of all, can Pravin Gordhan survive and succeed? This depends on whether he is *allowed* to survive and succeed, which is partly about Zuma's apparent determination to put his own interests above the country and its economy, and partly about whether the rest of the ANC leadership, Mantashe especially, is willing to continue to back Gordhan. I think Gordhan will survive and succeed because he will get sufficient backing and because Treasury is strong. Although it will be a fierce and bitter war, with battles won and lost on both sides, and with plenty of collateral damage principally to South Africa's economic prospects, Gordhan has enough aces in his pack to trump even Zuma's most deadly moves.

For the centre to hold – the sixth and final question – not only must Gordhan survive and succeed, but also a new social accord must be built in order to cushion South Africa from the undoubtedly bumpy socio-economic terrain it must traverse in the coming few years. It is precarious and uncertain. But, having looked over the precipice, South Africa may have the institutional wherewithal and human capital to pull itself back. The establishment is strong and has a lot to lose, and it will provide the steely resolve that some within the political leadership lack. If not, the plunge into a Brazil-like descent will be inevitable, and not just messy but thoroughly miserable.

Against this backdrop, the 'break scenario' is easier to describe. In it, Zuma prevails, while Gordhan fails and falls. The reform package is not delivered. The downgrade to junk status happens in December 2016. The economy spirals further downwards and we fall off the fiscal cliff. Painful cuts are made, with difficult and unanticipated political consequences. As a public-sector wage agreement is reneged, COSATU turns against the ANC, and the public service all but abandons its post. A Brazilian-style crisis of political leadership and economic disintegration beckons. As inflation rises and food becomes unaffordable, people starve. And then they protest, violently, led by a militant student movement with little to lose. A South African Spring arrives. The establishment fights back, though domestic capital has taken flight. More people die, as first the police and then the army fail to keep control without resorting to violence. Malema is martyred. A state of emergency is declared. It is 1985 all over again. The world looks on horrified, but too busy with its own crises to bother too much, though tourists now think thrice before they head this far south regardless of the collapsed rand. Now a very ordinary country, South Africa staggers along as a freshly elected, authoritarian populist drags us further down. He could be Mantashe. Or Zuma, again. Or someone else. By then it will no longer greatly matter.

The 'make scenario' is more difficult to articulate. The underlying constraints are not so easy to dislodge. And yet, to use that annoying cliché, there is plenty of low-hanging fruit to pluck. In this scenario, Pravin Gordhan prevails. He and the other reformers push

Zuma and his corrupt cronies into retreat. Business and government continue to talk, and the three working groups on avoiding a downgrade, creating a R4 billion fund for small- and medium-enterprise job creation, and overcoming the structural constraints to growth continue to make tangible progress. Treasury is able to finesse a fiscal path that avoids any serious cuts in public expenditure or tax hikes, and government waste is reduced. The public service raises its game, and at local government level the wake-up call of a tightly contested set of elections in August 2016 drives better performance, resulting in fewer social protests and more socio-economic stability. In turn, the ANC is propelled towards a return to its traditional, principled self, regrouping and recovering its progressive equilibrium point. Zuma is recalled and then reprosecuted. A new sense of public accountability is instilled and the days of impunity are ended. Cyril Ramaphosa succeeds Zuma and invokes the one-nation spirit of Mandela, rebuilding the social compact of the 1990s, inspiring unity as well as action as business and the wealthy classes give more. A new, more promising era of progress unfolds as market confidence is also restored and government makes greater strides in implementing a coherent national development plan across a better-led, better-coordinated administration.

Sound credible? As I said, it is harder to paint this scenario.

How will we be able to tell which path South Africa is taking? Here are nine signposts along the road:
1. Closely watch the socio-economic indicators relating to inflation, and especially food-price hikes, as the winter months unfurl and spring arrives, to note how they impact on social protest and whether they trigger a new student uprising in the spring.

2. See whether such instability and violence impacts on the 'strike season', which commences during the same period and which will have special relevance for the already beleaguered mining sector.

3. See what happens next, in terms of the new era of coalition politics. Can the DA put together the 'right' coalitions, ones that are durable and which don't undermine their ability to make their case as an alternative government? Or, more likely, does Julius Malema continue to destabilise politics and, through messy coalitions, city government?

4. In October 2016 the Medium Term Budget Policy Statement will tell us a lot about who is winning in the war between Pravin Gordhan and the president. Has Treasury been able to hold the line and stave off any corrupt intrusions on fiscal probity, such as an unaffordable nuclear deal? Moreover, is Gordhan surviving and succeeding?

5. In turn, this will determine whether South Africa has any chance of avoiding an investment-grade downgrade to junk status in December. By then, Gordhan will have had to have shown substantive progress in his checklist of reforms and that government's attempts with business and labour to spark some growth while building a new social compact are gaining real ground. A downgrade will prompt a Brazil-like descent; thus, avoiding it should provide a platform for greater stability and progress.

6. In terms of Zuma's own prospects and the ANC's unfolding succession race, by early 2017 we should know the Constitutional Court's view of the unlawfulness of the 2009 decision to discontinue charges against Zuma, and whether the court is willing to order the National Prosecuting Authority to proceed with the

charges or whether that delicate decision will be left in the distrusted hands of NDPP Shaun Abrahams. This, in turn, will tell us whether Zuma's grip on the main institutions of the criminal justice system remains as tight or has loosened somewhat as the end of the Zuma years approaches.

7. The start of the 2017 political year in February will be especially dramatic and important. The State of the Nation Address and the Budget Speech will reveal a great deal about the balance of power both in government and in the ANC, with implications for policy and the political trajectory of the country: will it be lurching in a more populist and authoritarian direction? In mid-2017, the ANC national policy conference, traditionally held around six months before its five-yearly national elective conference – unless a special elective conference has been called in the meantime – will provide further clues as to the direction of travel, especially in terms of whether Zuma intends to go for the 'Putin Option' of a third term as ANC president, compelled by his and his cronies' venal interests to try to control power from the back seat with a puppet state president.

8. The ANC national elective conference in December 2017 will bring to the West Wing either Cyril Ramaphosa or a more nationalist (Dlamini-Zuma) or populist (Mantashe) president, either in 2019 or more quickly, if the ANC decides at that point to dispense with the services of President Zuma.

9. Lastly, the 2019 national election will soon be upon us, though a great deal of water will have flowed under the bridge by then.

To return to the proverbial frog-in-the-pot metaphor, 9/12 spat the frog out. South Africa was given, in an entirely surprising way, a chance to break free from the rut of recent years. Since then, the frog has remained suspended tantalisingly above the close-to-boiling pot. It can't remain suspended indefinitely. Political gravity will pull it down. It will either fall back into the pot or land safely outside it. If the frog falls back in, then, in theory, it ought to notice and spring back out. Or perhaps it's too wounded and weary, and it simply, sadly, boils alive.

Notes

Introduction: Game on!

1. Richard Calland, *The Zuma Years* (Cape Town: Zebra Press, 2013), p. 169.
2. Qaanitah Hunter and Sibongakonke Shoba, 'Zuma told me to help Guptas', *Sunday Times*, 20 March 2016.

Chapter 1: The last frontier

1. Ngoako Ramatlhodi, 'ANC's fatal concessions', *Times Live*, 1 September 2011. Available at http://www.timeslive.co.za/opinion/commentary/2011/09/01/the-big-read-anc-s-fatal-concessions (last accessed 6 June 2016).
2. Richard Calland, 'Things Fall Apart; The Centre Cannot Hold', in K. Bentley, R. Calland & L. Nathan (eds), *Falls the Shadow: The Gap Between the Promise of the South African Constitution and the Reality* (Cape Town: UCT Press, 2013), p. 200.
3. Jay Naidoo, 'Stop insane attacks on our Constitution', JayNaidoo.org, 2011. Previously available at http://www.jaynaidoo.org/stop-insane-attacks-on-our-constitution (last accessed 9 November 2012).
4. Sipho Pityana, foreword to *Falls the Shadow: The Gap Between the Promise of the South African Constitution and the Reality*, p. vii.
5. Richard Calland, 'Nkandla fiasco reminiscent of arms deal mess', *Mail & Guardian*, 10 October 2014. Available at http://mg.co.za/article/2014-10-09-nkandla-fiasco-reminiscent-of-arms-deal-mess (last accessed 1 June 2016).
6. 'The Judiciary's Commitment to the Rule of Law', statement issued by the chief justice, the heads of court and senior judges of all divisions on 8 July 2015. Available at http://www.judiciary.org.za/doc/Statement-Issued-By-The-Chief-Justice_8-July-2015.pdf (last accessed 22 July 2015).

7. Natasha Marrian, 'Alliance resurrects Moseneke's Zuma criticism', *Business Day*, 2 July 2015. Available at http://www.bdlive.co.za/national/ politics/2015/07/02/alliance-resurrects-mosenekes-zuma-criticism (last accessed 6 June 2016). See also Alliance Summit Declaration, 1 July 2015. Available at http://www.anc.org.za/show.php?id=11528 (last accessed 3 July 2015).

8. See 'SACP Central Committee Report to the 3rd Special National Congress as delivered by the General Secretary Dr Blade Nzimande', 8 July 2015. Available at http://www.sacp.org.za/main.php?ID=4810 (last accessed 22 July 2015).

9. 'Nhleko questions independence of judiciary', *EWN*, 25 June 2015. Available at http://ewn.co.za/2015/06/25/First-On-EWN-Minister -Nathi-Nhleko-questions-independence-of-judiciary (last accessed 20 September 2015).

10. *Southern Africa Litigation Centre v Minister of Justice and Constitutional Development and Others* (27740/2015) [2015] ZAGPPHC 402 (24 June 2015). Available at http://www.saflii.org/za/cases/ZAGPPHC/2015/402 .html (last accessed 18 August 2015).

11. At his birthday party in January 2008, not long after the watershed ANC national conference at which Jacob Zuma was elected president of the ANC, Moseneke was reported to have said: 'I chose this job very carefully. I have another ten to twelve years on the bench and I want to use my energy to help create an equal society. It's not what the ANC wants or what the delegates want; it is about what is good for our people.' This prompted an angry reaction from parts of the ANC. See, for example, 'ANC takes issue with deputy chief justice', *Mail & Guardian Online*, 15 January 2008. Available at http://mg.co.za/article/ 2008-01-15-anc-takes-issue-with-deputy-chief-justice (last accessed 1 June 2016).

12. Ngcobo persuaded, as I recorded in *The Zuma Years*, then minister of justice Jeff Radebe to create a new department – the Office of the Chief Justice. But after his appointment as chief justice, Mogoeng found the government was dragging its heels on providing the budgetary means to create real autonomy for the OCJ. Mogoeng fought back and in 2015 won a victory with a R5.8 billion allocation of funds for a three-year

period of the medium-term budget. Although this is not 'new' money, in that it is essentially a reallocation of funds from the Department of Justice, it represents an important further step in permitting the judicial branch of government to establish administrative independence.

13. Niren Tolsi, 'Mogoeng, from pariah to saviour', *Mail & Guardian*, 15 April 2016. Available at http://mg.co.za/article/2016-04-14-mogoeng -from-pariah-to-saviour (last accessed 1 June 2016).

Chapter 2: David 3, Goliath 2

1. Mandy Rossouw, 'Zuma's R65m Nkandla splurge', *Mail & Guardian*, 4 December 2009. Available at http://mg.co.za/article/2009-12-04-zumas -r65m-nkandla-splurge (last accessed 20 April 2016).

2. Pierre de Vos, 'Nkandla report exposes President Zuma's personal involvement in the project', *Constitutionally Speaking*, 20 March 2014. Available at http://constitutionallyspeaking.co.za/nkandla-report -exposes-president-zumas-personal-involvement-in-the-project/ (last accessed 20 April 2016).

3. De Vos, 'Nkandla scandal: It was a simple choice between right and wrong', *Constitutionally Speaking*, 6 April 2016. Available at http://constitutionallyspeaking.co.za/nkandla-scandal-it-was-a-simple -choice-between-right-and-wrong/ (last accessed 20 April 2016).

4. The full text of the judgment is available here: https://s3-us-west-1 .amazonaws.com/eyewitnessnews/160331NkandlaJudgment.pdf (last accessed 21 April 2016).

5. Stefaans Brümmer, 'SCA judges slam Public Protector's Oilgate arguments', *Mail & Guardian*, 13 May 2011. Available at http://mg.co.za/ article/2011-05-13-supreme-court-judges-slam-public-protectors-oilgate -arguments (last accessed 21 April 2016).

6. See http://www.corruptionwatch.org.za/bua-mzansi-public-protector -campaign/ (last accessed 21 April 2016).

7. According to the latest Afrobarometer Survey, which was conducted in spring 2015, while trust in many government institutions, including the president, fell markedly in recent years, trust in the Office of the Public Protector remained 'stable', with 58 per cent of respondents trusting it somewhat or a lot. See http://afrobarometer.org/sites/default/files/

publications/Dispatches/ab_r6_dispatchno90_south_africa_trust_in
_officials.pdf (accessed 3 July 2016).

Chapter 3: Appointing judges, Malema-style

1. *My Vote Counts NPC v Speaker of the National Assembly and Others*
   (CCT121/14) [2015] ZACC 31 (30 September 2015). Available at
   http://www.saflii.org/za/cases/ZACC/2015/31.html (last accessed
   1 June 2016).
2. Calland, *The Zuma Years*, pp. 289–290.

Chapter 4: Game changer

1. Anyway Chingwete, 'In South Africa, citizens' trust in president,
   political institutions drops sharply', Afrobarometer Dispatch No. 90,
   17 May 2016. Available at http://afrobarometer.org/sites/default/files/
   publications/Dispatches/ab_r6_dispatchno90_south_africa_trust_in
   _officials.pdf (last accessed 8 June 2016).
2. 'A broken man, presiding over a broken society', speech delivered by
   DA parliamentary leader Mmusi Maimane MP, during the State of the
   Nation Address debate, 17 February 2015.

Chapter 5: What next for the ANC?

1. Richard Calland, *Anatomy of South Africa: Who Holds the Power?*
   (Cape Town: Zebra Press, 2006).
2. Susan Booysen, 'Zuma will go – but it won't be an easy task', *Mail &
   Guardian*, 21 April 2016. Available at http://mg.co.za/article/2016-04-21
   -zuma-will-go-but-it-wont-be-an-easy-task (last accessed 10 June 2016).
3. Natasha Marrian, 'Mabuza laughs off talk about a premier league',
   Business Day, 27 January 2016. Available at http://www.bdlive.co.za/
   national/politics/2016/01/27/mabuza-laughs-off-talk-about-a-premier
   -league (last accessed 10 June 2016).
4. Gareth van Onselen, 'Dlamini-Zuma and Serafina II: The original
   Nkandla', *Business Day*, 8 April 2016. Available at http://www.bdlive.co
   .za/opinion/columnists/2016/04/08/dlamini-zuma-and-sarafina-ii-the
   -original-nkandla (last accessed 21 July 2016).
5. Address by Deputy President Cyril Ramaphosa during Presidency

Budget Vote, National Assembly, 4 May 2016. Available at http://www.
thepresidency.gov.za/pebble.asp?relid=21995 (last accessed 9 June 2016).

Chapter 6: A delicate time, in a dangerous year …

1. When the SCA was subsequently attacked by some media
   commentators for erroneously attributing the phrase 'generally
   corrupt relationship' to Judge Squires, the SCA responded with a
   statement asserting that '[t]he trial court's view of the "symbiosis"
   between Mr Zuma and Mr Shaik was confirmed by the SCA in various
   parts of its judgment, which ultimately conveyed that on the evidence
   in this case an overall corrupt relationship existed'. See James Myburgh,
   'Zuma, the SCA and the "generally corrupt relationship" phrase',
   Politicsweb, 18 January 2015. Available at http://www.politicsweb.co.za/
   documents/zuma-the-sca-and-the-generally-corrupt-relationshi (last
   accessed 8 June 2016).

2. In a subsequent case, involving the controversial decision to drop
   serious criminal charges against the head of police intelligence, Richard
   Mdluli, Judge John Murphy gave a brilliant and brave judgment at first
   instance, holding that such decisions were covered by the wider PAJA
   review, but this was overturned by the SCA in 2014.

3. CASAC Media Statement, 29 April 2016. Available at https://www.
   facebook.com/CASACZA/posts/1047706131955982 (last accessed 8 June
   2016).

4. *Democratic Alliance v Acting National Director of Public Prosecutions and
   Others* (19577/2009) [2016] ZAGPPHC 255 (29 April 2016). Available at
   http://www.saflii.org/za/cases/ZAGPPHC/2016/255.html (last accessed
   9 June 2016).

5. In March 2011, crime intelligence boss Richard Mdluli was charged with
   the 1999 murder of Oupa Ramogibe, the husband of his former lover.
   In September, he was charged separately for fraud and corruption
   relating to his alleged abuse of crime intelligence's secret service
   account. By the following year, however, acting National Director of
   Public Prosecutions Nomgcobo Jiba had withdrawn all the charges. In
   September 2013, Judge John Murphy ruled in the Pretoria High Court
   that the various criminal charges against Mdluli must be reinstated.

Mdluli and the NPA were given leave to appeal Murphy's decision, but in April 2014, the Supreme Court of Appeal upheld the High Court's ruling and ordered that the criminal charges be reinstated.

Chapter 7: Risk on, risk off

1. Rene Vollgraaff, 'South Africa current-account deficit widens as exports drop', *Bloomberg*, 8 March 2016. Available at http://www.bloomberg .com/news/articles/2016-03-08/south-africa-current-account-gap-widens -to-5-1-as-exports-drop (last accessed 9 June 2016).
2. Pravin Gordhan, 'We can do much to spur growth in economy', *Sunday Times*, 24 April 2016.
3. 2016 Budget Speech, by Pravin Gordhan, Minister of Finance, delivered on 24 February 2016. Available at http://www.treasury.gov.za/documents/ national%20budget/2016/speech/speech.pdf (last accessed 3 May 2016).
4. Christo Wiese, Cas Coovadia and Colin Coleman, 'SA has 3 months to save itself', *Sunday Times*, 13 March 2016. Available at http://www. timeslive.co.za/sundaytimes/opinion/2016/03/13/SA-has-3-months-to -save-itself (last accessed 9 June 2016).
5. Natasha Marrian, Allan Seccombe and Carol Paton, 'New Mineral Resources Minister Mosebenzi Zwane riles ANC, industry', *Business Day*, 25 September 2015. Available at http://www.bdlive.co.za/national/ politics/2015/09/25/new-mineral-resources-minister-mosebenzi-zwane -riles-anc-industry (last accessed 9 June 2016).

Chapter 8: Will the centre hold?

1. Karl von Holdt et al., 'The smoke that calls: Insurgent citizenship, collective violence and the struggle for a place in the new South Africa. Eight case studies of community protest and xenophobic violence', Centre for the Study of Violence and Reconciliation, July 2011. Available at http://www.csvr.org.za/docs/thesmokethatcalls.pdf (last accessed 25 May 2016).
2. M. Shaw and K. Thomas, 'The commercialisation of assassination: "Hits" and contract killing in South Africa, 2000–2015', *African Affairs*, forthcoming, 2016.
3. Gareth van Onselen, 'Political assassinations: How the ANC is killing

its own', *Business Day*, 12 August 2013. Available at http://www.bdlive.co
.za/opinion/columnists/2013/08/12/political-assassinations-how-the-anc
-is-killing-its-own (last accessed 25 May 2016).

Index

By the same author

The face of power in South Africa is rapidly changing – for better and for worse.

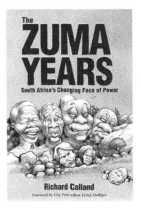

The years since Thabo Mbeki was swept aside by Jacob Zuma's 'coalition of the wounded' have been especially tumultuous, with the rise and fall of populist politicians such as Julius Malema, the terrible events at Marikana, and the embarrassing Guptagate scandal.

- What lies behind these developments?
- How does the Zuma presidency exercise its power?
- Who makes our foreign policy?
- What goes on in cabinet meetings?
- What is the state of play in the Alliance – is the SACP really more powerful
- than before?
- As the landscape shifts, what are the opposition's prospects?

In *The Zuma Years*, Richard Calland attempts to answer these questions, and more, by holding up a mirror to the new establishment; by exploring how people such as Malema, Chief Justice Mogoeng Mogoeng and DA parliamentary leader Lindiwe Mazibuko have risen so fast; by examining key drivers of transformation in South Africa, such as the professions and the universities; and by training a spotlight on the toxic mix of money and politics.

The Zuma Years is a fly-on-the-wall, insider's approach to the people who control the power that affects us all. It takes you along the corridors of government and corporate power, mixing solid research with vivid anecdote and interviews with key players. The result is an accessible yet authoritative account of who runs South Africa, and how, today.

Do you have any comments, suggestions or
feedback about this book or any other Zebra Press titles?
Contact us at **talkback@zebrapress.co.za**

*

Visit **www.randomstruik.co.za** and subscribe
to our newsletter for monthly updates and news